The Art of War

The Art of War
A NEW TRANSLATION

TRANSLATION, ESSAYS
AND COMMENTARY BY

The Denma Translation Group

SHAMBHALA
Boston & London
2001

Shambhala Publications, Inc.
Horticultural Hall
300 Massachusetts Avenue
Boston, Massachusetts 02115
www.shambhala.com

9 8 7 6 5 4

Printed in the United States of America

♾ This edition is printed on acid-free paper that meets the American
National Standards Institute z39.48 Standard.

Distributed in the United States by Random House, Inc., and in
Canada by Random House of Canada Ltd

Library of Congress Cataloging-in-Publication Data
Sun-tzu, 6th cent. B.C.
[Sun-tzu ping fa. English]
The art of war: a new translation / translation, essays and
commentary by The Denma Translation Group.
p. cm.
Includes index.
ISBN 1-57062-552-2
1. Military art and science—Early work to 1800. I. Title.
U101'.S9513 2001
355.02—dc21
00-058330

To the Dorje Dradül of Mukpo

Contents

The Art of War

INTRODUCTION

Applying *The Art of War*

ABOUT 2,300 YEARS AGO IN WHAT IS NOW NORTH CHINA, A lineage of military leaders put their collective wisdom into written form for the first time. Their text was to shape the strategic thinking of all East Asia. It offered a radically new perspective on conflict, whereby one might attain victory without going to battle. Though in the West their text is called *The Art of War*, in China it is still known as the *Sun Tzu*, named for the patriarch of their lineage.

Over the last half-century, this text has become a handbook for people all around the world seeking to transform their approach to conflict, whether in warfare, in business or simply in everyday life. When a squadron leader targets his objective or a boardroom falls under siege, when our neighbors join a zoning battle to protect local parkland, we may find modern-day warriors turning to the *Sun Tzu*. Clearly they have a conviction that its ancient wisdom has considerable value today. But how might we apply this Chinese text to our lives in a genuine manner? How can it teach us to work more effectively with conflict? These are the central questions of this book.

The answers lie within the *Sun Tzu* itself. The text shows how to conquer without aggression, whether our conflict is large or small, personal or national. One of its most famous couplets states:

One hundred victories in one hundred battles is not
the most skillful.
Subduing the other's military without battle is the
most skillful.

The wisdom of this book is a profound human knowledge,
something to which every one of us has access. It does not belong
to any proprietary group, Chinese or Western. It shows a way of
working with conflict that is sane, kindly and effective. Though
the *Sun Tzu* offers models of behavior, it does not suggest we copy
them. Instead, it invites us to enter its teachings fully. When we
do so, we find we come naturally to the same insights that are
contained within its text.

The *Sun Tzu* begins with the understanding that conflict is an
integral part of human life. It is within us and all around us.
Sometimes we can skillfully sidestep it, but at other times we
must join with it directly. Many of us have seen the destructive
power of aggression, whether on a personal level or in the disasters
of armed conflict. We know as well the limitations of most political and personal responses to that aggression. How can we work
with it in a more profound and effective way?

The *Sun Tzu* recommends that our response to conflict start
from knowledge, of ourselves and of the other. In chapter 3 it says:

And so in the military—
Knowing the other and knowing oneself,
In one hundred battles no danger.
Not knowing the other and knowing oneself,
One victory for one loss.
Not knowing the other and not knowing oneself,
In every battle certain defeat.

Self-knowledge in the *Sun Tzu* includes awareness of the full
condition of our forces, but it begins with something far more

Introduction

intimate: knowledge of our own minds. People come to this knowledge in many ways. The contemplative practices offer one means of insight. More basic than any particular practice, though, is the openness of mind to which it leads. This openness can be present in all our activities. We find ourselves there when we experience a sudden moment of beauty. It is the unformed, creative source of the performing and plastic arts. Athletes know it as "the zone," and lovers do not even name it. It is where they are most at home and their actions most effective.

Why, though, would anyone wary of aggression's destructive force study a text about conflict? As the *Sun Tzu* says, it is essential to know ourselves, to know our own minds. But we also live in a world where aggression cannot be avoided. We must know the other in order to skillfully engage him or her. It is necessary, therefore, to learn to work directly with the conflict in our environment, not ignore it, submerge it, give up on it or try to deny its existence. However profound our individual wisdom, it will not survive in the world unless it is joined with some kind of power. Recognizing this seems especially important at the present time, when the consequences of human action can be so thoroughly devastating. This text, then, shows how we can work with conflict both within and outside ourselves.

THE MILITARY LINEAGE that brought *The Art of War* into the world traced itself back to a master strategist named Sun Tzu. According to legend, he had been celebrated for brilliant campaigns conducted around the time of Confucius, in the sixth century BCE. This work of military strategy was passed on to subsequent lineage holders, at first by memorization and laborious copying on bamboo strips. Gradually its wisdom became known to outsiders, and increasingly it circulated throughout ancient China. We know it was sought by early emperors, for the imperial library catalog of the first century BCE lists a copy in its collection. The text's reputation spread from China throughout East Asia, and the figure of Sun Tzu came to represent the supreme model of strategic thinking.

Through what process, though, are we to make a genuine connection with this ancient work from so far away, learning to practice from the heart of its tradition rather than simply admiring or mimicking it? We are aided here by the example of the sage commander, the general to whom the *Sun Tzu* is addressed. He embodies the worldview of the text, and his example allows us to see the full range of its activity. Though when taken together his achievements may seem extraordinary, every one of his qualities is already present in each of us. Such abilities grow naturally from our native capacities to see, hear, think and interact with the world.

The English language still asks us to choose between masculine and feminine pronouns. Because Chinese generals have historically been men, we have adopted the convention of referring to the sage commander throughout as "he." It is central to our understanding, however, that the knowledge and action of the sage commander are the property of neither male nor female. The wisdom of the *Sun Tzu* applies not just to men in a military setting but to anyone seeking to work with conflict without aggression.

We recognize the qualities of the sage commander in certain unusual women and men. They may have a remarkable calm about them, or they appear endlessly resourceful. At the same time, it is possible that such people have never heard of the *Sun Tzu*. Their examples demonstrate the way in which the wisdom found in this text is not a foreign import but is instead a natural flowering of common human faculties.

If we seek the root of the sage commander's power, we discover that he is simply and genuinely himself, always comfortable with who he is. The more he relaxes, the greater the power associated with him. In some people such openness may arise quite spontaneously. Or they may develop it from a strong discipline, or out of the sharp and sudden experience of seeing through the hold that fear has upon the human mind.

From this fearlessness the sage commander develops an appreciation of the world around him. He no longer regards things as for or against him but sees them with dispassionate judgment.

He holds to no fixed position or identity. Thus his wisdom emerges in the moment, on the spot.

The *Sun Tzu* repeatedly stresses that such wisdom is the root of skillful action. It is the first of the general's four qualities (chapter 1). It determines the difference between victory and defeat. Thus in chapter 10 the text says:

> Knowing my troops can strike, yet not knowing the
>   enemy cannot be struck.
> This is half of victory.
> Knowing the enemy can be struck, yet not knowing
>   my soldiers cannot strike.
> This is half of victory.
> Knowing the enemy can be struck, knowing my
>   soldiers can strike, yet not knowing that the
>   form of the earth cannot be used to do battle.
> This is half of victory.

This knowing begins with the visible details of troop strength and supply but develops through these to encompass the Tao-like complexity of events, which the great general also knows. It includes insight into the extraordinary and orthodox manifestations of battle and brings with it the ability to feel at home in chaos.

How do we apply this knowledge? There are many opportunities for it, even in our most routine domestic life. A mother asks her child to go to bed. The child, no doubt for good reasons of his own, refuses. If the mother refrains from action, her son may not get the sleep he needs and may suspect that he can refuse all future commands. However, if she presses straight ahead, the mother only bolsters her son's resistance. What is the right course of action? How does she bring about the desired effect without creating a bigger war and a less workable home life?

First of all, we cannot expect to advise the parent in the abstract, except in the broadest sense. Skillful action emerges only from knowledge of all the details that go to make up the situation. In other words, we are on our own, as each new life situation arises. No person, no book, no external wisdom can tell us how to act. Even previously successful models cannot simply be laid over the unique realities of our present situation. As chapter 1 of the *Sun Tzu* says,

> These are the victories of the military lineage.
> They cannot be transmitted in advance.

Thus we must determine the means for victory now and here, since its conditions exist only in the moment.

Furthermore, we all recognize a mother's feeling for her child, and each of us can see that our enemy is human, just as we are. This wisdom does not originate in some external source. Rather, it is insight we all possess. It requires no unusual talent, nothing that is not already ours. We need only our human intelligence, attention to the moment and openness to the world. At the same time, we can also develop all of these abilities.

Approaching the *Sun Tzu* in this way, we see that its teachings are not limited to any single realm of activity. Its language can apply equally to the mother putting her son to bed and to a platoon commander resisting his superior officer's disastrous order to fight the wrong opponent. The *Sun Tzu* works at the level of the battle of ego or of warfare between nations, and everything between. Yet its specific application can only come from the uniqueness of a particular case.

This uniqueness has far-reaching implications for how one studies the text and practices it in real-life situations. It means that the present translation of the *Sun Tzu* can be only one part of a complex process. The text contains the words, and the words set out the nature of conflict, providing us with a host of models. But only when we have gone beyond its specific words, concepts and examples will we be free to respond openly and accurately to the life situation that is arising before, around and within us.

It is helpful to this process if we can identify the perspective of the *Sun Tzu*, seeing the world the way it does. Above all, this is the view of "taking whole." Taking whole means conquering the enemy in a way that keeps as much intact as possible—both our own resources and those of our opponent. Such a victory leaves something available on which to build, both for us and for our former foe. This is not merely a philosophical stance or altruistic approach. Destruction leaves only devastation, not just for those defeated, their dwellings and their earth, but also for conquerors attempting to enforce their "peace" long after battle has passed. True victory is victory over aggression, a victory that respects the enemy's basic humanity and thus renders further conflict unnecessary.

Taking whole begins with the ordinary details of our lives. It includes all of them. The mother trying to put her son to bed must know his habits, temperament and disposition as well as her own, how these vary throughout the day and what special factors are at play that particular evening. Sensing their configuration, her actions shift with and respond to these changing conditions. Throughout, she seeks a larger perspective.

That larger perspective is so powerful that it subtly brings other people around to a view they cannot initially see—her son, our enemy, our reluctant allies. It is both powerful and attractive because it includes them in a way they recognize, which is accommodating, beyond petty concerns, and respecting of their own intelligence and perspective. This is not simply about bringing the other person over to your side but bringing him or her to something larger than either side. This view is always there. It comes with considerable responsibility.

Taking whole is both a way of being and a way of seeing. Because our actions arise naturally out of it, it is also a way of acting. It does not preclude the use of force, but in using force, it seeks to preserve the possibilities—to keep the options open and include the welfare of the other. It leads ultimately to victory.

One manifestation of taking whole is a victory that occurs without battle. But winning without fighting is not simply an alternative way to reach our objective, this time without expending valuable resources. It is a fundamentally different understanding of the ground of conflict. It resembles "win-win," in which each party gains what it needs. But victory goes beyond the particular desires of either side to a larger vision. Thus it applies both to friendly negotiations between equals and to unequal forces caught in bitter conflict. This victory carries tremendous power, since it owes no loyalty to smaller reference points.

Victory embraces all aspects of the world. Rejecting parts of it means that we have given up on the workability of the situation and are left with force as the only option. That perpetuates the struggle, in ourselves and all around us. It solidifies a view of the other as our opposite and of conflict as win or lose. It makes us susceptible to defeat, since it captures our mind, closes off our perceptions of the world and prevents a full knowledge from arising.

HOWEVER APPEALING this vision of victory, it is still true that the *Sun Tzu* was written very long ago by people whose world was vastly different from ours. If we wish to study their text, how can we find its essential teachings while still acknowledging that they arose at a unique time and place? We cannot simply ignore these differences and decide that their ideas mean whatever we would like.

This is a question about linkage through time and space, between the foreign and the familiar. It is also about lineage. Once, the book belonged to certain people. Now, we are claiming, it can belong to us. A better understanding of the nature of how the text arose and what it meant in the world of its first users will help us see how the text could belong to our world today.

Scholars believe that the *Sun Tzu* emerged from the oral tradition sometime in the fourth century BCE at a time when Chinese models of governance, warfare, morality and social organization were experiencing extreme dislocation. Endemic warfare had destroyed confidence in the old ways. The widest variety of solutions was proposed,

SHAMBHALA PUBLICATIONS, INC.

MAILING LIST
P.O. BOX 308, BACK BAY ANNEX
BOSTON, MASSACHUSETTS   02117-0308

SHAMBHALA

 SHAMBHALA PUBLICATIONS

If you wish to receive a copy of the latest Shambhala Publications catalogue of books and to be placed on our mailing list, please send us this card — or send us an e-mail at info@shambhala.com

Please print

BOOK IN WHICH THIS CARD WAS FOUND..

NAME..

ADDRESS..

CITY.. STATE ....

ZIP OR POSTAL CODE .... COUNTRY..
(if outside U.S.A.)

E-MAIL ADDRESS..

Detach bookmark before mailing card

from revival of traditional forms to a hard-edged organizational efficiency useful to the formation of large armies and impersonal bureaucracies.

The response of the *Sun Tzu* was to emphasize that knowledge arises in the present moment. Any form could be helpful—but its application depends on insight into one's present circumstances, into the nowness of the situation. Such knowledge, the text argues, "cannot be transmitted in advance."

Thus the *Sun Tzu* does not organize its thought into systematic procedures we might follow. Now, when we read a book, we often find it helpful to seek out its essential principles, extracting them and then generalizing from them, applying them skillfully to new situations. This can be an extremely powerful and efficient way to acquire and structure new knowledge. But though the *Sun Tzu* does contain a few principles, such as "not transmitted in advance," it mostly offers us examples that concretely embody the point of view from which it regards the world. It is a loosely linked set of observations and models, with only the barest argumentation connecting them. It does not develop its doctrines through logical demonstration. Rather, it teaches by analogy and metaphor. We cannot simply pluck its insights and drop them into our already existing frameworks. We must develop new ways to use our minds.

Our book therefore offers a variety of approaches to the *Sun Tzu*. It is not necessary to read it straight through. Some readers may want to begin with the three essays in the middle that introduce its thought and practice. The first of these essays, "Taking Whole," presents the worldview of the text, showing its implications for working with the present moment. It develops the idea of Tao as a way of being, seeing and doing. The second, "The Sage Commander," gives a fuller vision of the central figure of the book, whom we have briefly described above. It suggests a view of this fully developed person in order to spark the recognition of these qualities in ourselves. The third, "Joining the Tradition," explores just how and why an ancient text has the possibility of meeting our current world. Part of the reason lies in the *Sun Tzu* itself and part in the fundamental remaking of the Western worldviews that has occurred over the last hundred years.

Qualities of the Chinese language also suggested a particular translation strategy. When we first read English-language versions of the *Sun Tzu* in the 1970s, we were convinced, like many others, that it might contain enormous power. Yet we were frustrated, since its wisdom often seemed concealed in paraphrase. Going to the original Chinese, we were astounded by its simplicity, clarity and bluntness. It stopped one's mind midthought. We had a definite conviction that it should be possible to reproduce these qualities in English. It was also clear why other translations had filled in many words and explanations: the text could be extremely difficult, sometimes confusing even its Chinese commentators.

Our translation, then, aims to preserve the naked quality of the text, to reproduce the sound and feel of the Chinese and thus capture the moment when the *Sun Tzu* was first emerging from the oral tradition. To do so, we have forged a lithic, unadorned English, halfway between prose and poetry. Its simplicity encourages a reader to approach the book without undue reliance on concept, allowing its sounds, patterns and meaning to seep into the mind. As we remove the filters between ancient text and modern reader, the *Sun Tzu* begins to reveal itself directly to us.

This translation therefore makes intense demands on its readers, asking them to contemplate the text and dwell in its repetitive quality, not seeking abstract principles nor resolving its inconsistencies. Like certain other classics of China—the *Lao Tzu* and *I Ching* come to mind—it is often pithy, epigrammatic and pregnant with implications, yet somewhat obscure on first or second reading. This is as true for Chinese readers as it is for us. The users of all these texts have therefore required some assistance in understanding them. This may be supplied through an oral tradition, represented by a living teacher. Or it may take written form, appearing as commentary and even subcommentary.

The *Sun Tzu* is an example of this tradition. Dozens of commentaries were written on it, and ten of the most famous from the third to the eleventh centuries are usually printed together with the Chinese text. The best English-language source for these is Samuel Griffith's 1963 translation, which relies on them to clarify the implications of many passages.[1]

We have instead provided our own commentary. In keeping with Chinese tradition, we supply information an English-speaking reader will need to understand the *Sun Tzu*—background material from language and history and a discussion of key terms on their first appearance. Our goal is to remove barriers between reader and text.

But whereas traditional commentaries go on from this to establish definitive meanings, our commentary points to the view of the whole, so that people's understanding may deepen naturally. The text of the *Sun Tzu* is so compressed that it supports a variety of plausible interpretations. We have refrained from specific interpretations because they limit the range of meaning that the text can communicate. This is not just a theoretical preference but a conviction that arises from our experience working with people over the last decade. We have been impressed by the insights of relatively inexperienced readers, who have found significant meaning in the *Sun Tzu* with only an elementary orientation to the text.

There are a number of ways that we invite you to explore the *Sun Tzu* beyond the reading and contemplation of this book. Some people may wish to mix private study with more public discussions about the text's meaning and application. Our Web site, www.victoryoverwar.com, provides this opportunity. Here we have put together a study guide for reading groups that will aid in delving deeper into the text. It also contains alternative essays on the *Sun Tzu*, born with the writing of this book but represented in it only indirectly.

The Web site has as well a large section in which we discuss the meaning range of individual words, present arguments regarding the interpretation of each passage, note parallels with other ancient texts and consider these ideas against China's broader history. In addition we explain the choices we have made in translation. We have also included the entire Chinese text of the *Sun Tzu* and its word-by-word English rendering. Because Chinese and English word orders are very similar, even someone lacking any knowledge of Chinese can learn to follow the text in both languages. These materials constitute the full scholarly apparatus of our book.

WE BELIEVE that the *Sun Tzu* contains a profound ordinary wisdom, that it teaches taking whole. In this book we show how one might make a genuine connection with it, learning a more skillful approach to the conflict that arises inevitably in our daily life. We can do so because this way of being does not belong solely to the *Sun Tzu*. It is basic human knowledge, the wisdom of nonaggression.

Thus every modern reader of the text may forge a relationship to the *Sun Tzu* similar to that of Chinese readers over the last two millennia. This is how we enter the tradition. No one can say in advance what the text will mean to us. Though it offers models of behavior we might emulate, we can do so successfully only when we understand its underlying view from the inside, mixing our own mind with its wisdom.

Then, in situations of conflict, its pith instructions begin to shape the way we think and act. What seemed like foreign truths become recognizable as our own. Our actions become a natural expression of what the world is and how it works. This is the ground for practicing the art of war.

Introduction

PART ONE

Sun Tzu's
The Art of War

IN SOME INSTANCES THIS TRANSLATION MAY RESIST IMMEDIATE understanding. Readers may therefore wish to consult the commentary in Part Three of this book, in which we provide a range of information helpful in working with the text.

Passages that rhyme in Chinese are indicated by a ~ placed at the end of a line. We have used the mark § to indicate where we believe section breaks occur in the text, but the original Chinese contains neither punctuation nor paragraphing.

I

Appraisals

SUN TZU SAID:

The military is a great matter of the state.
It is the ground of death and life,
The Tao of survival or extinction.
One cannot but examine it.

§

And so base it in the five.
Compare by means of the appraisals.
Thus seek out its nature.

The first is Tao, the second is heaven, the third is
  earth, the fourth is the general, the fifth is
  method.

Tao is what causes the people to have the same
  purpose as their superior.
Thus they can die with him, live with him and
  not deceive him.

Heaven is *yin* and *yang*, cold and hot, the order
  of the seasons.

Going with it, going against it—this is military
 victory.

Earth is high and low, broad and narrow, far and
 near, steep and level, death and life.

The general is knowledge, trustworthiness,
 courage and strictness.

Method is ordering divisions, the Tao of ranking
 and principal supply.

As for all these five—
 No general has not heard of them.
 Knowing them, one is victorious.
 Not knowing them, one is not victorious.

§

And so compare by means of the appraisals.
Thus seek out its nature.
Ask—
 Which ruler has Tao?
 Which general has ability?
 Which attains heaven and earth?
 Which implements method and orders?
 Whose military and multitudes are strong?
 Whose officers and soldiers are trained?
 Whose rewards and punishments are clear?
By these I know victory and defeat!

The general heeds my appraisals. Employ him and
 he is certainly victorious. Retain him.
The general does not heed my appraisals. Employ
 him and he is certainly defeated. Remove
 him.

§

Having appraised the advantages, heed them.
Then make them into *shih* to aid with the external.
Shih is governing the balance according to the
    advantages.

§

The military is a Tao of deception—
    Thus when able, manifest inability.
    When active, manifest inactivity.
    When near, manifest as far.
    When far, manifest as near.
    Thus when he seeks advantage, lure him. ∾
    When he is in chaos, take him. ∾
    When he is substantial, prepare against him. ∾
    When he is strong, avoid him. ∾
    When he is wrathful, harass him.
    Attack where he is unprepared.
    Emerge where he does not expect it.

These are the victories of the military lineage.
They cannot be transmitted in advance.

§

Now, in the rod-counting at court before battle, one
    is victorious who gets many counting rods.
In the rod-counting at court before battle, one is
    not victorious who gets few counting rods.
Many counting rods is victorious over few counting
    rods,
How much more so over no counting rods.
By these means I observe them.
Victory and defeat are apparent.

2

Doing Battle

SUN TZU SAID:

In sum, the method of employing the military—

With one thousand fast chariots, one thousand
    leather-covered chariots and one hundred
    thousand armored troops to be provisioned
    over one thousand *li*—
then expenses of outer and inner, stipends of
    foreign advisers, materials for glue and
    lacquer, and contributions for chariots and
    armor are one thousand gold pieces a day.
Only after this are one hundred thousand soldiers
    raised.

§

When one employs battle—
    If victory takes long, it blunts the military and
        grinds down its sharpness.
    Attacking walled cities, one's strength is
        diminished.
    If soldiers are long in the field, the state's
        resources are insufficient.

Now if one blunts the military, grinds down its
        sharpness,
Diminishes its strength and exhausts its goods,
Then the feudal lords ride one's distress and rise up.
Even one who is wise cannot make good the
        aftermath!

Thus in the military one has heard of foolish speed
        but has not observed skillful prolonging.
And there has never been a military prolonging
        that has brought advantage to the state.

§

And so one who does not thoroughly know the
        harm from employing the military ～
Cannot thoroughly know the advantage from
        employing the military. ～

§

One skilled at employing the military
Does not have a second registering of conscripts nor
        a third loading of grain.
One takes equipment from the state and relies on
        grain from the enemy.
Thus the army's food can be made sufficient.

§

A state's impoverishment from its soldiers—
    When they are distant, there is distant transport.
    When they are distant and there is distant
        transport, the hundred clans are impoverished.
    When soldiers are near, things sell dearly.
    When things sell dearly, wealth is exhausted.
    When wealth is exhausted, people are hard-
        pressed by local taxes.

Diminished strength in the heartland,
Emptiness in the households.
Of the hundred clans' resources, six-tenths is gone.
Of the ruling family's resources—
    Broken chariots, worn-out horses, ∾
    Armor, helmets, arrows, crossbows, ∾
    Halberds, shields, spears, pavises, ∾
    Heavy ox-drawn wagons— ∾
  Seven-tenths is gone.

Thus the wise general looks to the enemy for food.
One bushel of enemy food equals twenty bushels of
    mine.
One bale of fodder equals twenty bales of mine.

§

And so killing the enemy is a matter of wrath.
Taking the enemy's goods is a matter of advantage.

§

And so in chariot battles—
    When more than ten chariots are captured,
    Reward him who first captures one.
    Then change their flags and pennants.
    When the chariots are mixed together, ride them.
    Supply the captives and care for them.
This is what is meant by "victorious over the enemy
    and so increasing one's strength."

§

And so the military values victory.
It does not value prolonging.

§

And so the general who knows the military is the
    people's fate star,
The ruler of the state's security and danger.

3

Strategy of Attack

SUN TZU SAID:

In sum, the method of employing the military—

Taking a state whole is superior.
Destroying it is inferior to this.

Taking an army whole is superior.
Destroying it is inferior to this.

Taking a battalion whole is superior.
Destroying it is inferior to this.

Taking a company whole is superior.
Destroying it is inferior to this.

Taking a squad whole is superior.
Destroying it is inferior to this.

Therefore, one hundred victories in one hundred
    battles is not the most skillful.
Subduing the other's military without battle is the
    most skillful.

§

And so the superior military cuts down strategy.
Its inferior cuts down alliances.
Its inferior cuts down the military.
The worst attacks walled cities.

§

The method of attacking walled cities—
    Ready the siege towers and armored vehicles.
    This is completed after three months.
    Pile up the earthworks.
    This also takes three months.
    If the general is not victorious over his anger
        and sets them swarming like ants,
    One-third of the officers and soldiers are killed
        and the walled city not uprooted—
    This is the calamity of attack.

§

And so one skilled at employing the military
    Subdues the other's military but does not do
        battle,
    Uproots the other's walled city but does not
        attack,
    Destroys the other's state but does not prolong.
One must take it whole when contending for all-
        under-heaven.
Thus the military is not blunted and advantage can
        be whole.
This is the method of the strategy of attack.

§

And so the method of employing the military—
    When ten to one, surround them.
    When five to one, attack them.

When two to one, do battle with them.
When matched, then divide them.
When fewer, then defend against them.
When inadequate, then avoid them.
Thus a small enemy's tenacity ∾
Is a large enemy's catch. ∾

§

Now the general is the safeguard of the state.
If the safeguard is complete, the state is surely
    strong.
If the safeguard is flawed, the state is surely weak.

§

And so the sovereign brings adversity to the army
    in three ways—

    Not knowing the army is unable to advance yet
        ordering an advance,
    Not knowing the army is unable to retreat yet
        ordering a retreat,
    This is what is meant by "hobbling the army."

    Not knowing affairs within the three armies yet
        controlling the governance of the three
        armies,
    Then the army's officers are confused!

    Not knowing the three armies' balance yet
        controlling appointments in the three armies,
    Then the army's officers are distrustful!

Once the three armies are confused and distrustful,
Troubles from the feudal lords intensify!
This is what is meant by "an army in chaos leads to
    victory."

§

And so knowing victory is fivefold—
> Knowing when one can and cannot do battle is
> victory.
> Knowing the use of the many and the few is
> victory.
> Superior and inferior desiring the same is
> victory.
> Being prepared and awaiting the unprepared is
> victory.
> The general being capable and the ruler not
> interfering is victory.

These five are a Tao of knowing victory.

§

And so in the military—
> Knowing the other and knowing oneself, ∾
> In one hundred battles no danger. ∾
> Not knowing the other and knowing oneself, ∾
> One victory for one loss. ∾
> Not knowing the other and not knowing
> oneself, ∾
> In every battle certain defeat. ∾

4

Form

Of old the skilled first made themselves invincible
   to await the enemy's vincibility.

Invincibility lies in oneself.
Vincibility lies in the enemy.

Thus the skilled can make themselves invincible.
They cannot cause the enemy's vincibility.

Thus it is said, "Victory can be known. It cannot be
   made."

§

Invincibility is defense.
Vincibility is attack.

Defend and one has a surplus.
Attack and one is insufficient.

Of old those skilled at defense hid below the nine
        earths and moved above the nine heavens.
Thus they could preserve themselves and be
        all-victorious.

§

In seeing victory, not going beyond what everyone
        knows is not skilled.
Victory in battle that all-under-heaven calls skilled
        is not skilled.
Thus lifting an autumn hair does not mean great
        strength.
Seeing the sun and the moon does not mean a clear
        eye.
Hearing thunder does not mean a keen ear.
So-called skill is to be victorious over the easily
        defeated.
Thus the battles of the skilled are without
        extraordinary victory, without reputation for
        wisdom and without merit for courage.

§

And so one's victories are without error.
Being without error, what one arranges is
        necessarily victorious
Since one is victorious over the defeated.

One skilled at battle takes a stand in the ground of
        no defeat
And so does not lose the enemy's defeat.
Therefore, the victorious military is first victorious
        and after that does battle.
The defeated military first does battle and after that
        seeks victory.

§

And so one who is skilled cultivates Tao and
        preserves method.
Thus one can be the measure of victory and defeat.

§

As for method—
    First, measure length.
    Second, measure volume.
    Third, count.
    Fourth, weigh.
    The fifth is victory.

    Earth gives birth to length.
    Length gives birth to volume.
    Volume gives birth to counting.
    Counting gives birth to weighing.
    Weighing gives birth to victory.

§

A victorious military is like weighing a
        hundredweight against a grain.
A defeated military is like weighing a grain against
        a hundredweight.
One who weighs victory sets the people to battle
        like releasing amassed water into a gorge one
        thousand *jen* deep.

This is form.

5

Shih

Ordering the many is like ordering the few.
It is division and counting.

Fighting the many is like fighting the few.
It is form and name.

The multitude of the three armies can be made to
      meet all enemies without defeat.
It is the extraordinary and the orthodox.

How a military comes to prevail, like throwing a
      grindstone against an egg.
It is the empty and the solid.

§

In sum, when in battle,
Use the orthodox to engage.
Use the extraordinary to attain victory.

§

And so one skilled at giving rise to the
      extraordinary—

As boundless as heaven and earth,
As inexhaustible as the Yellow River and the
    ocean.

Ending and beginning again,
It is the sun and the moon.

Dying and then being born,
It is the four seasons.

§

Musical pitches do not exceed five,
Yet all their variations cannot be heard.

Colors do not exceed five,
Yet all their variations cannot be seen.

Tastes do not exceed five,
Yet all their variations cannot be tasted.

The shih of battle do not exceed the extraordinary
    and the orthodox,
Yet all their variations cannot be exhausted.

The extraordinary and the orthodox circle and give
    birth to each other,
As a circle has no beginning.
Who is able to exhaust it?

§

The rush of water, to the point of tossing rocks
    about. This is shih.
The strike of a hawk, at the killing snap. This is the
    node.

Therefore, one skilled at battle—
    His shih is steep.
    His node is short.

Shih is like drawing the crossbow.
The node is like pulling the trigger.

§

Pwun-pwun. Hwun-hwun.
The fight is chaotic yet one is not subject to chaos.

Hwun-hwun. Dwun-dwun.
One's form is round and one cannot be defeated.

Chaos is born from order.
Cowardice is born from bravery.
Weakness is born from strength.

Order and chaos are a matter of counting.
Bravery and cowardice are a matter of shih.
Strength and weakness are a matter of form.

§

One skilled at moving the enemy
    Forms and the enemy must follow,
    Offers and the enemy must take.
Move them by this and await them with troops.

§

And so one skilled at battle
Seeks it in shih and does not demand it of people.
Thus one can dispense with people and employ
        shih.

One who uses shih sets people to battle as if rolling
        trees and rocks.
As for the nature of trees and rocks—
    When still, they are at rest.
    When agitated, they move.

When square, they stop.
When round, they go.
Thus the shih of one skilled at setting people to
battle is like rolling round rocks from a
mountain one thousand *jen* high.

This is shih.

6

The Solid and Empty

One who takes position first at the battleground
  and awaits the enemy is at ease.
One who takes position later at the battleground
  and hastens to do battle is at labor.
Thus one skilled at battle summons others and is
  not summoned by them.

How one can make the enemy arrive of their own
  accord—offer them advantage.
How one can prevent the enemy from arriving—
  harm them.
Thus how one can make the enemy labor when at
  ease and starve when full—emerge where
  they must hasten.

§

To go one thousand li without fear, go through
  unpeopled ground.
To attack and surely take it, attack where they do
  not defend.
To defend and surely hold firm, defend where they
  will surely attack.

Thus with one skilled at attack, the enemy does not
      know where to defend.
With one skilled at defense, the enemy does not
      know where to attack.

§

Subtle! Subtle!
To the point of formlessness. ～
Spiritlike! Spiritlike!
To the point of soundlessness. ～
Thus one can be the enemy's fate star. ～

§

To advance so that one cannot be resisted, charge
      against the empty.
To retreat so that one cannot be stopped, go so far
      that one cannot be reached.

And so if I wish to do battle, the enemy cannot but
      do battle with me.
I attack what he must save.

If I do not wish to do battle, I mark a line on the
      earth to defend it, and the enemy cannot do
      battle with me.
I misdirect him.

§

And so the skilled general forms others yet is
      without form.
Hence I am concentrated and the enemy is divided.
I am concentrated and thus one.
The enemy is divided and thus one-tenth.
This is using one-tenth to strike one.

When I am few and the enemy is many, I can use
      the few to strike the many because those with
      whom I do battle are restricted!

The ground on which I do battle with him cannot
      be known.
Then the enemy's preparations are many.
When his preparations are many, I battle the few!

Prepare the front and the rear has few.
Prepare the left and the right has few.
Everywhere prepared, everywhere few.

The few are those who prepare against others.
The many are those who make others prepare
      against them.

§

Knowing the battle day and knowing the
      battleground,
One can go one thousand li and do battle.
Not knowing the battle day and not knowing the
      battleground,
The front cannot help the rear, the rear cannot
      help the front,
The left cannot help the right, the right cannot
      help the left.
How much more so when the far is several tens of li
      and the near is several li away!

§

Though by my estimate the military of Yueh is
      many,
How does this further victory?

Thus it is said, "Victory can be usurped."
Although the enemy is numerous, they can be kept
from fighting.

§

And so prick them and know the pattern of their
movement and stillness.
Form them and know the ground of death and life.
Appraise them and know the plans for gain and
loss.
Probe them and know the places of surplus and
insufficiency.

§

The ultimate in giving form to the military is to
arrive at formlessness.
When one is formless, deep spies cannot catch a
glimpse and the wise cannot strategize.

Rely on form to bring about victory over the
multitude,
And the multitude cannot understand.
The elite all know the form by which I am
victorious,
But no one knows how I determine the form of
victory.
Do not repeat the means of victory,
But respond to form from the inexhaustible.

Now the form of the military is like water.
Water in its movement avoids the high and hastens
to the low.
The military in its victory avoids the solid and
strikes the empty.

Thus water determines its movement in accordance
with the earth.
The military determines victory in accordance with
the enemy.
The military is without fixed shih and without
lasting form.

To be able to transform with the enemy is what is
meant by "spiritlike."

Of the Five Phases, none is the lasting victor.
Of the four seasons, none has constant rank.
The sun shines short and long.
The moon dies and lives.

Spiritlike essentials.

7

The Army Contending

In sum, the method of employing the military—

The general receives the command from the
      sovereign,
Joins with the army, gathers the multitude,
      organizes them and encamps.
Nothing is more difficult than an army contending.

The difficulty for a contending army
Is to make the circuitous direct
And to make the adverse advantageous.

Thus make their road circuitous
And lure them with advantage.
Setting out later than others and arriving sooner
Is knowing the appraisals of circuitous and direct.

§

A contending army brings advantage.

A contending army brings danger.
Contending for advantage with an entire army, one
     will not get there.
Contending for advantage with a reduced army,
     one's baggage train is diminished.

Therefore, rolling up one's armor, hastening after
     advantage day and night without camping,
     continually marching at the double for one
     hundred li and then contending for
     advantage—
   The commander of the three armies is captured.
   The strong ones sooner, the worn-out ones later,
     and one in ten arrives.
Going fifty li and contending for advantage—
   The ranking general falls.
   By this method half arrive.
Going thirty li and contending for advantage—
   Two-thirds arrive.
Therefore—
   An army without a baggage train is lost,
   Without grain and food is lost,
   Without supplies is lost.

§

Therefore—
   Not knowing the strategies of the feudal lords,
   One cannot ally with them.
   Not knowing the form of mountains and forests,
     defiles and gorges, marshes and swamps,
   One cannot move the army.
   Not employing local guides,
   One cannot obtain the advantage of the ground.

§

And so the military is based on guile,
Acts due to advantage,
Transforms by dividing and joining.

§

And so—
    Swift like the wind,
    Slow like the forest,
    Raiding and plundering like fire,
    Not moving like a mountain,
    Difficult to know like yin,
    Moving like thunder.

§

When plundering the countryside, divide the
    multitude.
When expanding territory, divide the advantage.
Weigh it and act.

§

One who knows in advance the Tao of the
    circuitous and direct is victorious.
This is the method of the army contending.

§

Therefore, the *Governance of the Army* says—
    "Because they could not hear each other, they
        made drums and bells.
    Because they could not see each other, they
        made flags and pennants."

Therefore—
    In day battle use more flags and pennants.
    In night battle use more drums and bells.
Drums and bells, flags and pennants are the means
    by which one unifies the ears and eyes of the
    people.

Once the people have been tightly unified,
The brave have no chance to advance alone,
The cowardly have no chance to retreat alone.
This is the method of employing the many.

§

And so the *ch'i* of the three armies can be seized.
The heart-mind of the commander can be seized.

Therefore, morning ch'i is sharp, midday ch'i is lazy,
        evening ch'i is spent.
Thus one skilled at employing the military
Avoids their sharp ch'i and strikes their lazy and
        spent ch'i.
This is ordering ch'i.

Use order to await chaos.
Use stillness to await clamor.
This is ordering the heart-mind.

Use the near to await the far.
Use ease to await labor.
Use fullness to await hunger.
This is ordering strength.

Do not engage well-ordered pennants.
Do not strike imposing formations.
This is ordering transformation.

§

And so the method of employing the military—
    Do not face them when they are on a high hill.
    Do not go against them with their back to a
        mound.
    Do not pursue them when they feign defeat.

Leave a way out for surrounded soldiers. ⌇
Do not block soldiers returning home. ⌇
This is the method of employing the many.

Four hundred sixty-five.

8

The Nine Transformations

SUN TZU SAID:

In sum, the method of employing the military—

The general receives the command from the
   sovereign,
Joins with the army and gathers the multitude.

§

In spread-out ground do not encamp.
In junction ground join with allies.
In crossing ground do not linger.
In enclosed ground strategize.
In death ground do battle.

§

There are roads one does not follow.
There are armies one does not strike.
There are cities one does not attack.
There are grounds one does not contest.
There are commands of the sovereign one does
   not accept.

§

And so the general who comprehends the
 advantages of the nine transformations
Knows how to employ the military!
The general who does not comprehend the
 advantages of the nine transformations,
Though knowing the form of the ground, is unable
 to obtain the advantages of the ground!
When one orders the military but does not know
 the teachings of the nine transformations,
Though knowing the five advantages, one is unable
 to employ people!

§

Therefore—
 The plans of the wise necessarily include
  advantage and harm.
 They include advantage. Thus one's service can
  be trusted.
 They include harm. Thus adversity can be
  undone.

Therefore—
 Subdue the feudal lords with harm.
 Occupy the feudal lords with tasks.
 Hasten the feudal lords with advantage.

§

And so the method of employing the military—
 Do not rely on their not coming.
 Rely on what we await them with.
 Do not rely on their not attacking.
 Rely on how we are unable to be attacked.

§

And so for the general there are five dangers—
    Resolved to die, one can be killed.
    Resolved to live, one can be captured.
    Quick to anger, one can be goaded.
    Pure and honest, one can be shamed.
    Loving the people, one can be aggravated.
All five are the excesses of the general,
A calamity in employing the military.

To overturn an army and kill the general,
One must use the five dangers.
One cannot but examine them.

9

Moving the Army

SUN TZU SAID:

In sum, positioning the army and scrutinizing the
    enemy—

In crossing mountains,
    Hold to the valleys.
    Look out at life ground and take a high position.
    Battle downhill. Do not ascend.
This is positioning the army in mountains.

In crossing water,
    One must distance oneself from it.
    When the invader approaches across water, do
        not meet him in the water.
    To order a strike when he is half across is
        advantageous.
    When wishing to do battle,
    Do not go close to the water to meet the invader.
    Look out at life ground and take a high position.
    Do not go against the current.
This is positioning the army by water.

In crossing salt marshes,
  Be sure to leave quickly. Do not linger.
  If one encounters an army in the midst of a salt
    marsh,
  Hold to the water grass and keep one's back to
    the trees.
This is positioning the army in salt marshes.

On plains
  Take a position on level ground.
  Keep the high to the right and back.
  In front, death. Behind, life.
This is positioning the army on plains.

All four are the advantages of the army, how the
    Yellow Emperor was victorious over the Four
    Emperors.

§

In sum, the army likes the high and hates the low,
Values yang and disdains yin,
Sustains life and takes a position in the solid.
This is what is meant by "surely victorious."
The army is without the hundred afflictions.

In hills and dikes, take a position in yang.
Keep them to the right and back.
This is the advantage of the military, the assistance
    of the earth.

When it has rained upstream, the stream's flow
    intensifies.
Stop fording. Wait for it to calm.

When crossing heavenly ravines, heavenly wells,
    heavenly prisons, heavenly nets, heavenly
    sinkholes and heavenly fissures,
One must quickly leave them. Do not go near.
When I am far from them, the enemy is near them.
When I face them, the enemy has his back to them.

When alongside the army are defiles, ponds, reeds,
    small forests and dense vegetation that can
    conceal people,
Search these carefully and repeatedly.
They are where the devious take position.

When the enemy is near and still, he is relying on
    the steep.
When the enemy is far and provokes battle, he
    wishes the other to advance—
    He is occupying the level and advantageous.

§

Many trees move.
He is approaching.

Many obstacles in thick grass.
He is misleading us.

Birds rise up.
He is concealing himself.

Animals are startled.
He is launching a total assault.

§

Dust is high and sharp.
Chariots are approaching.

It is low and wide.
The infantry is approaching.

It is dispersed and wispy.
The firewood gatherers are approaching.

It is scattered here and there.
He is encamping his army.

§

His words are humble and his preparations increase.
He will advance.

His words are strong and his advance is forced.
He will retreat.

Light chariots come out first and take a position on
        the flank.
He is deploying.

He is not in difficulty yet requests peace.
He is strategizing.

They rush out to deploy.
He has set the moment.

Half of them advance.
He is luring you.

§

They lean on their weapons.
They are hungry.

Those who draw water drink first.
They are thirsty.

They see advantage but do not advance.
They are tired.

Birds gather.
It is empty.

They call out at night.
They are afraid.

The encampment is disorderly.
The general has no weight.

Flags and pennants are moved about.
There is chaos.

Officers are angry.
They are fatigued.

They feed grain to their horses and eat meat, the
    army does not hang up their water pots, and
    they do not return to their quarters.
The invaders are exhausted.

§

He repeatedly and soothingly speaks to his men in
    measured tones.
He has lost the multitude.

There are many rewards.
He is in distress.

There are many punishments.
He is in difficulty.

At first he is harsh and later fears the multitude.
He is utterly unskillful.

He approaches with gifts and entreaties.
He wishes to rest.

The military is wrathful and faces one for a long
        time without either engaging or withdrawing.
One must carefully examine this.

§

In the military more is not better.

Do not advance in a martial way.
It is sufficient to gather strength, assess the enemy
        and take him—that is all.

However, if one does not plan and takes the enemy
        lightly,
One will certainly be captured by him.

§

If the troops do not yet feel close kinship with one
        and they are punished, they will not submit.
If they do not submit, they are difficult to employ.
If the troops already feel close kinship with one and
        punishments are not carried out, do not
        employ them.

And so assemble them by fellowship,
Make them uniform by the martial.
This is what is meant by "certain to seize it."

If one acts consistently to train the people, the
        people will submit.

If one acts inconsistently to train the people, the people will not submit.
One who acts consistently is in accord with the multitude.

Moving the Army   39

10

Forms of the Earth

SUN TZU SAID:

The forms of the earth—
 open, hung, stalled, narrow, steep and distant.

I am able to go. He is able to come. This is called
  "open."
As for the open form—
 Be first to occupy the high and yang.
 Secure your supply routes.
 If I do battle, it is advantageous.

I can go but it is difficult to return. This is called
  "hung."
As for the hung form—
 When the enemy is unprepared, I emerge and
  am victorious over him.
 When the enemy is prepared, if I emerge and am
  not victorious,
 It is difficult to return.
 It is not advantageous.

I emerge and it is not advantageous. He emerges
      and it is not advantageous. This is called
      "stalled."
As for the stalled form—
    Although the enemy offers me advantage, I do
      not emerge. I lead my troops away.
    To order a strike when half the enemy has
      emerged is advantageous.

As for the narrow form—
    If I occupy it first, I must fill it and await the
      enemy.
    If the enemy occupies it first and fills it, do not
      pursue.
    If he does not fill it, pursue.

As for the steep form—
    If I occupy it first, I must occupy the high and
      yang and await the enemy.
    If the enemy occupies it first, I lead the troops
      away.
    Do not pursue.

As for the distant form—
    Since shih is equal, it is difficult to provoke battle.
    To do battle is not advantageous.

All these six are a Tao of the earth,
The general's utmost responsibility.
One cannot but examine them.

§

And so in the military there is driven off, the bow
      unstrung, dragged down, the mountain
      collapsing, chaos and routed.

All these six are not a calamity of heaven.
They are the excesses of the general.

Now shih is equal and he uses one to strike ten.
This is called "driven off."

The troops are strong and the officers weak.
This is called "the bow unstrung."

The officers are strong and the troops weak.
This is called "dragged down."

A great officer is wrathful and does not submit.
When he encounters the enemy,
He is filled with rancor and does battle on his own.
The general does not know his ability.
This is called "the mountain collapsing."

The general is weak and not strict.
His training and leadership are not clear.
The officers and troops are inconstant.
The formations of the military are jumbled.
This is called "chaos."

The general cannot assess the enemy.
With the few he engages the many.
With the weak he strikes the strong.
The military is without elite forces.
This is called "routed."

All these six are a Tao of defeat,
The general's utmost responsibility.
One cannot but examine them.

§

Now forms of the earth are an assistance to the
    military.
Assess the enemy and determine victory.
Appraise the steep and level, the far and near.
This is a Tao of the superior general.
One who knows these and employs battle is
    certainly victorious.
One who does not know these and employs battle is
    certainly defeated.

§

And so when according to the Tao of battle there is
    certain victory and the ruler says do not do
    battle, one can certainly do battle.

When according to the Tao of battle there is no
    victory and the ruler says one must do battle,
    one can not do battle.

§

And so he advances yet does not seek fame.
He retreats yet does not avoid blame.
He seeks only to preserve the people,
And his advantage accords with that of the ruler.
He is the treasure of the state.

He looks upon the troops as his children.
Thus they can venture into deep river valleys
    with him.
He looks upon the troops as his beloved sons.
Thus they can die together with him.

He is generous yet unable to lead.
He is loving yet unable to give orders.
He is chaotic and unable to bring order.

They are like spoiled children.
They cannot be employed.

§

Knowing my troops can strike, yet not knowing the
       enemy cannot be struck.
This is half of victory.

Knowing the enemy can be struck, yet not knowing
       my soldiers cannot strike.
This is half of victory.

Knowing the enemy can be struck, knowing my
       soldiers can strike, yet not knowing that the
       form of the earth cannot be used to do battle.
This is half of victory.

§

And so one who knows the military
Acts and is not confused,
Initiates and is not exhausted.

§

And so it is said—
    Know the other and know oneself, ∾
    Then victory is not in danger. ∾
    Know earth and know heaven, ∾
    Then victory can be complete. ∾

The Nine Grounds

SUN TZU SAID:

The method of employing the military—

There is dispersed ground, light ground, contested
    ground, connected ground, junction ground,
    heavy ground, spread-out ground, enclosed
    ground and death ground.

The feudal lords battle for this ground.
This is "dispersed."

I enter another's ground, but not deeply.
This is "light."

If I obtain it, it is advantageous. If he obtains it, it is
    also advantageous.
This is "contested."

I am able to go. He is able to come.
This is "connected."

Where the grounds of three feudal lords meet, the
    one who arrives first will obtain the multitudes
    of all-under-heaven.
This is "junction."

I enter another's ground deeply, with many walled
    cities and towns at my back.
This is "heavy."

I move through mountains, forests and swamps—in
    sum, roads difficult to move along.
This is "spread-out."

The way by which I exit and enter is narrow.
The way by which I pursue and return is circuitous.
His few can strike my many.
This is "enclosed."

If quick, I survive.
If not quick, I am lost.
This is "death."

Therefore—
    In dispersed ground do not do battle.
    In light ground do not stop.
    In contested ground do not attack.
    In connected ground do not cross.
    In junction ground join with allies.
    In heavy ground plunder.
    In spread-out ground move.
    In enclosed ground strategize.
    In death ground do battle.

§

In ancient times those called skilled at battle were
    able to prevent—

The enemy's van and rear from reaching each
    other, ∾
The many and the few from relying on each
    other, ∾
Noble and base from helping each other, ∾
Superior and inferior from coordinating with
    each other, ∾
Separated troops from regrouping, ∾
The assembled military from becoming uniform. ∾

§

If it accords with advantage, then act.
If it does not accord with advantage, then stop.

§

Dare one ask,
    "The enemy, amassed and in good order, is about
        to approach.
    How do I await him?"
I say,
    "Seize what he loves, and he will heed you!"

§

It is the nature of the military that swiftness rules.
Ride others' inadequacies.
Go by unexpected ways.
Attack where he has not taken precautions.

§

In sum, the Tao of being an invader—

    Enter deeply and one is concentrated.
    The defenders do not subdue one. ∾

    Plunder rich countryside.
    The three armies have enough to eat. ∾

Carefully nourish and do not work them.
Consolidate ch'i and accumulate strength. ∼

Move the military about and appraise one's
    strategies.
Be unfathomable. ∼

Throw them where they cannot leave.
Facing death, they will not be routed. ∼
Officers and men facing death, ∼
How could one not obtain their utmost strength? ∼

When military officers are utterly sinking, they do
        not fear. ∼
Where they cannot leave, they stand firm. ∼
When they enter deep, they hold tightly. ∼
Where they cannot leave, they fight. ∼

Therefore, they are—
    Untuned yet disciplined, ∼
    Unsought yet obtained, ∼
    Without covenant yet in kinship,
    Without orders yet trusting. ∼

    §

Prohibit omens, remove doubt, and even death
        seems no disaster.

    §

My officers do not have surplus wealth.
It is not that they hate goods.
They do not have surplus deaths.
It is not that they hate longevity.

On the day that orders are issued,

The tears of seated officers moisten their lapels,
The tears of those reclining cross their cheeks.

Throw them where they cannot leave—
It is the bravery of Chuan Chu and Ts'ao Kuei.

§

And so one skilled at employing the army may be
    compared to the *shuai-jan.*
The shuai-jan is a snake of Mount Heng.
Strike its head and the tail arrives.
Strike its tail and the head arrives.
Strike its midsection and both head and tail arrive.

Dare one ask,
    "Can one then make them like the shuai-jan?"
I reply,
    "One can. The people of Yueh and the people of
        Wu hate each other.
    When they are in the same boat crossing the river,
    They help each other like the left and right hand."

§

Therefore, tying horses together and burying wheels
Is not enough to rely on.

Make bravery uniform.
This is a Tao of governance.

Attain both hard and soft.
This is a pattern of earth.

§

And so one skilled at employing the military takes
    them by the hand as if leading a single person.

They cannot hold back.

§

In his activity ∾
The commander is tranquil and thus inscrutable,
Orthodox and thus brings order. ∾
He is able to stupefy the ears and eyes of officers
        and troops,
Preventing them from having it. ∾

He changes his activities, ∾
Alters his strategies,
Preventing the people from discerning. ∾

He changes his camp, ∾
Makes his route circuitous, ∾
Preventing the people from obtaining his plans. ∾

The leader sets the time of battle with them, ∾
Like climbing high and removing the ladder. ∾
The leader enters with them deep into the land of
        the feudal lords, ∾
Pulling the trigger. ∾

Like driving a flock of sheep,
He drives them there,
He drives them here, ∾
No one knows where they are going. ∾

He gathers the multitude of the three armies
And throws them into the defile.

This is what is meant by "the activity of the
        commander."

§

The variations of the nine grounds,
The advantages of contracting and extending,
The patterns of human nature—
One cannot but examine them.

§

In sum, being an invader—
　　Deep then concentrated,
　　Shallow then dispersed.

To leave the state and go over the border with
　　soldiers. This is crossing ground.
Four ways in. This is junction ground.
To enter deeply. This is heavy ground.
To enter shallowly. This is light ground.
Unyielding at the back, narrow in front. This is
　　enclosed ground.
Unyielding at the back, enemy in front. This is
　　death ground.
No way to leave. This is exhaustion ground.

Therefore—
　　In dispersed ground I will unify their will.
　　In light ground I will make them come together.
　　In contested ground I will keep them from
　　　　lingering.
　　In connected ground I will make firm my ties.
　　In junction ground I will be careful of what I
　　　　rely on.
　　In heavy ground I will hasten to bring up my rear.
　　In spread-out ground I will advance along his
　　　　roads.
　　In enclosed ground I will block the gaps.

In death ground I will show them that we will
    not live.

§

And so the nature of the feudal lords—
    When enclosed, they resist.
    When there is no holding back, they fight.
    When overcome, they follow.

Therefore—
    Not knowing the strategies of the feudal lords,
    One cannot ally with them.
    Not knowing the form of mountains and forests,
        defiles and gorges, marshes and swamps,
    One cannot move the army.
    Not employing local guides,
    One cannot obtain the advantage of the ground.
    Not knowing one of these four or five,
    One is not the military of the kings and
        overlords.

The military of those kings and overlords—
    If they attack a great state, then its multitude is
        unable to gather together.
    Their awesomeness spreads over the enemy, and
        his allies cannot assemble.

Therefore—
    Do not contend for allies in all-under-heaven.
    Do not cultivate balance in all-under-heaven.
    Trust in self-interest.
    Spread one's awesomeness over the enemy.
Thus his state can be seized and his walled cities
    can be made to submit.

§

Without method's rewards, ~
Without proper orders, ~
Bind the multitude of the three armies ~
As if leading a single person. ~

Bind them with deeds. Do not command them with
    words.
Bind them with harm. Do not command them with
    advantage.

Mire them in the ground of extinction and still
    they survive.
Sink them in death ground and still they live.

Now the multitude is sunk in harm, ~
Yet still they are able to make defeat into victory. ~

§

And so conducting the affairs of the military ~
Lies in carefully discerning the enemy's purpose. ~
Concentrate strength in one direction. ~
Go one thousand li and kill his general. ~
This is what is meant by "skillful deeds."

§

Therefore, on the day the policy is initiated— ~
    Close the passes and break the tallies.
    Do not let their emissaries pass. ~
    Hone it in the upper court
    In order to fix the matter. ~

§

When the enemy opens the outer gate, ～
One must quickly enter. ～
Make what he loves the first objective.
Hide the time of battle from him. ～
Discard the ink line and respond to the enemy ～
In order to decide the matter of battle. ～

Therefore—
    At first be like a virgin. ～
    The enemy opens the door. ～
    Afterward be like an escaped rabbit. ～
    The enemy will be unable to resist. ～

12

Attack by Fire

SUN TZU SAID:

In sum, there are five attacks by fire—
    The first is called "setting fire to people."
    The second is called "setting fire to stores."
    The third is called "setting fire to baggage trains."
    The fourth is called "setting fire to armories."
    The fifth is called "setting fire in tunnels."

Making fire has requisites.
The requisites must be sought out and prepared.

There is a season for setting fires.
There are days for starting fires.
The season is when heaven is dry.
The days are when the lunar mansion is the
        Winnowing Basket, the Wall, the Wings, and
        the Chariot Platform.
All four lunar mansions are days when the wind rises.

If fire is set inside, respond immediately from the
        outside.

If fire is set and his military is still, do not attack.
Rush to where the fire is calamitous.
If one can pursue them, then pursue.
If one cannot pursue, then stop.

If fire can be set outside, do not wait to set it inside.
Set it according to the season.
If fire is set upwind, do not attack from downwind.
If during the day wind is prolonged, at night the
      wind will stop.
One must know the variations of the five fires.
Use counting to watch for the time.

And so one who uses fire to aid an attack is
      dominant. ∾
One who uses water to aid an attack is strong. ∾
Water can be used to cut off. ∾
It cannot be used to seize. ∾

§

Now battle for victory, attack and attain it.
But if one does not follow up on the achievement,
      it is inauspicious.
One's fate is "wealth flowing away."

Thus it is said—
    The enlightened ruler contemplates it.
    The good general follows up on it.

If it is not advantageous, do not act.
If it is not attainable, do not employ troops.
If it is not in danger, do not do battle.

The ruler cannot raise an army on account of wrath.
The general cannot do battle on account of rancor.

If it accords with advantage, then employ troops.
If it does not, then stop.

Wrath can return to joy.
Rancor can return to delight.
An extinguished state cannot return to existence.
The dead cannot return to life.
Thus the enlightened sovereign is careful about this.
The good general is cautious about this.

These are a Tao of securing the state and keeping
    the army whole.

13

Employing Spies

SUN TZU SAID:

In sum—
When raising one hundred thousand soldiers and
setting out on a campaign of one thousand li,
the expenses of the hundred clans and the
contributions of the nation are one thousand
gold pieces a day.
Inner and outer are disturbed.
People are exhausted on the roads.
Seven hundred thousand households are unable to
manage their affairs.

On guard against them for years to contend for a
single day's victory, yet, by begrudging rank
and the reward of a hundred gold pieces, he
does not know the nature of the enemy.
He is utterly inhumane.
He is not the general of the people.
He is not the assistant of the ruler.
He is not the ruler of victory.

§

And so the means by which an enlightened
        sovereign and a wise general act, and so are
        victorious over others and achieve merit
        superior to the multitude's—
This is foreknowledge.

    Foreknowledge cannot be grasped from ghosts
        and spirits,
    Cannot be inferred from events,
    Cannot be projected from calculation.
    It must be grasped from people's knowledge.

§

And so there are five kinds of spy to employ.
There is the native spy, the inner spy, the turned
        spy, the dead spy and the living spy.
When the five spies arise together and no one
        knows their Tao,
This is what is meant by "spiritlike web."
It is the treasure of the people's sovereign.

The living spy returns and reports.
Employ the native spy from among the local people.
Employ the inner spy from among their officials.
Employ the turned spy from among enemy spies.
The dead spy spreads false information abroad.
        I order my spy to know it, and he transmits
        it to the enemy spy.

§

And so, in the kinship of the three armies—
    No kinship is more intimate than that of a spy.
    No reward is more generous than that for a spy.
    No affair is more secret than that of a spy.

If not a sage, one cannot employ spies.
If not humane, one cannot send out spies.
If not subtle and secret, one cannot obtain a spy's
    treasure.

Secret! Secret!
There is nothing for which one cannot employ spies.

When the affairs of a spy are heard before they are
    under way,
The spy and those who have been told all die.

§

In sum,
The army one wishes to strike, the walled city one
    wishes to attack and the person one wishes to
    kill—
One must first know the family name and given
    name of the defending general, his intimates,
    the steward, the gatekeeper and attendants.
I order my spy to surely seek them out and know
    them.

I must seek out the enemy's spies who come to spy
    on me.
Accordingly, I benefit them, direct them and then
    release them.
Thus a turned spy can be obtained and employed.

With this knowledge the local spy and the inner
    spy can thus be obtained and sent out.
With this knowledge the dead spy thus spreads false
    information and can be sent to tell the enemy.
With this knowledge the living spy can thus be sent
    out on time.

One must know the matter of the five spies.
Knowing it surely lies in the turned spy.
Thus one cannot but be generous with a turned spy.

§

When Yin arose, I Chih was in Hsia.
When Chou arose, Lü Ya was in Yin.

Only if the enlightened ruler and wise general can
    use people of superior knowledge as spies will
    they surely achieve great merit.

These are essentials of the military.
The three armies rely on them and act.

PART TWO

Three Essays

ABOVE ALL, THE SUN TZU SHOWS A WAY OF CONQUERING WITHOUT aggression. It teaches victory over war. This is a way of seeing and a way of being, a point of view and equally a means of action. Our translation transposes the text from Chinese into English, while the commentary clarifies many issues of language and interpretation. These make it possible for us to approach the *Sun Tzu* and understand its words and meaning. But to enter the tradition still more deeply, we must learn how to assume its point of view.

These essays seek to assist in that process. They show the *Sun Tzu* in three aspects: its central insight, which is taking whole; its central figure, the sage commander; and the historical circumstances from which it emerged. These three converge to create a ground on which we may recognize the natural wisdom of the text. They show us how to move from a set of ancient words to a way of seeing and acting in the present.

The first essay describes how the *Sun Tzu* views the world as whole. It begins with the minutest of details, noting their interconnectedness. Then it identifies the patterns they form and the opportunities for effective action these afford. In particular, it develops the idea of shih, which is simultaneously a configuration of forces and the power inherent within them. Knowing these, we can engage in taking whole.

The *Sun Tzu* is addressed to the general, portrayed throughout as a sage commander. Our second essay describes his being and his activity, building an image of this wisdom as it is embodied in a human being. His achievements seem extraordinary. He also engages in activity such as deception that stands outside the bounds of conventional morality. This essay places all these actions in the context of victory and taking whole.

The *Sun Tzu* arose at a particular time and place, in response to specific historical conditions, and we are far removed from all that. By examining how it assumed its present form, we will see why it is not merely the exclusive property of an ancient lineage. In the course of this, we will discover the opportunities it offers us to join its tradition. Developments of the last century have created an environment particularly well suited to sustain this vision.

The text contains a profound ordinary wisdom. Our goal throughout is to show how one might enter the *Sun Tzu* so thoroughly that it evokes the same insights in us. Thus we can take up its genuine practice.

Taking Whole

THE SIMPLEST WAY TO ENTER THE SUN TZU IS TO IDENTIFY ITS POINT of view, the perspective from which it sees things. When we find that view, its world opens before us, and we can more readily identify its parts, their relationship and our own role within them.

That view is simple to name: the *Sun Tzu* sees the world whole, composed of a multitude of shifting, interrelating aspects. This is not only a way of seeing; it is a way of acting. Thus one of its best-known statements reads:

> Taking a state whole is superior.
> Destroying it is inferior to this. [Chapter 3]

We can begin to understand this perspective by examining the things closest to us, the ordinary objects of our lives. These interact in ever-shifting ways, of which we also form a part. As we start to sense their configurations, our own actions become synchronized with this. Being connected to the details, moving with their shapes and conformation, we can find victory.

The Nature of Things

At the start, we are dealing with the smallest details, visible, countable items, things that depend on the good ordering of noncommissioned officers: rice and rifles, maps, data on comparative troop strength. Taking whole means every single one of these. It extends as well to other items not so countable: morale, terrain, local weather patterns. Each one is relevant, everything that is part of that world, since all have weight in situations of battle. Thus chapter 1 lists implements, supply, ranking, punishments and the general's trustworthiness. Chapter 2 details some specific expenses in raising an army: "stipends of foreign advisers, materials for glue and lacquer, and contributions for chariots and armor."

This is necessary not only because each piece is relevant to combat. Every one of them also affects all the others. Altering a single piece, the movement of the whole also shifts. Undermine the general's trustworthiness, and a small rainstorm becomes a threatening torrent. Chapter 2, on economy, makes this very clear:

> A state's impoverishment from its soldiers—
>> When they are distant, there is distant transport.
>> When they are distant and there is distant
>>> transport, the hundred clans are
>>> impoverished.
>> When soldiers are near, things sell dearly.
>> When things sell dearly, wealth is exhausted.
>> When wealth is exhausted, people are hard-
>>> pressed by local taxes.

Because all things are interconnected, you must know each one, and how each one affects and effects every other. Only then can you plan effectively.

We are looking now at a sequence of events, so that when soldiers are near, things sell dearly, and thus wealth is exhausted and people hard-pressed. But that causal chain is already intersecting with another—for example, when it rains too much, then crops mildew and rot, and soothsayers and magicians are called in; thus people's trust shifts away from elders and officials, and the potential for peasant revolt intensifies.

All these sequences occur simultaneously. Everything is in touch with everything else, always in movement. We ordinarily understand certain sectors of our world to operate in this manner: prices fluctuate due to complex interactions of supply and demand. But what if everything were like that—a mobile of countless pieces, revolving at different speeds, so that its overall pattern were never the same? The parts of our mobile also change in relative weight, as one piece grows or shrinks, with balances always in adjustment.

This is the world of the *Sun Tzu*. It's the world not only of the *Sun Tzu* but also of ancient China, a set of shared assumptions about how things work. Different schools of thought emphasized different aspects of it, the Confucians seeking to order it through ritual and the cultivation of virtue and Taoists going with its flow. But all acknowledged it as the nature of their world.

Relationships

How do we work with this world? First of all, we must measure it from where we ourselves are standing. Here is a seemingly trivial example from a recent Chinese children's book, in which a squirrel is trying to figure out whether it is safe to cross a stream. To him, it is a raging current, and he will drown there. But the stream is only up to the fetlocks of a horse. This is not a question of definitions; it's a matter of how to act effectively in the world. We must determine whether it's appropriate for our platoon to cross the water. Here we cannot rely on information from the horse or squirrel: we must insert ourselves into the process of measurement, gauge ourselves in comparison to its elements. Thus what we are in any situation—for example, "able to cross" or "not able to cross"—is only partially a function of our relative size. What matters is how we fit the situation—whether we are big in *that* water. The answer we get will be very different from the answer someone else gets.

There are many examples of this way of thinking from the time of Sun Tzu. These two are from one of his main detractors, an influential Confucian named Hsün Tzu (310–220?), who lived perhaps a century after the compilation of the text. Hsün Tzu devotes a chapter to attacking the *Sun Tzu*, yet his thinking is entirely consonant with it on that point. This is what he says about positioning oneself:

> There is a plant in the western regions called the blackberry lily. Its stem is four inches long, but because it grows atop tall mountains, it looks down into a thousand-foot abyss.[1]

Assuming the right position, we can see vast distances, however limited our own person may be. Here it's as if the squirrel were riding on the horse's back.

Another of Hsün Tzu's examples, also from chapter 1 of his works, emphasizes the power that derives from this way of seeing:

> If you climb to a height and beckon, it's not that your arm grows longer, but it is seen from farther away. If you yell downwind, it's not that the sound gets swifter, but it is heard more clearly.

If we take advantage of certain qualities of the environment, our power greatly increases. To do so, we must appraise not just the object but how it will interact with other objects and situations—that is, we must know its relationships. Recall that in this world we are not a thing in and of ourselves; we have qualities like height or bravery only in contrast with other things. Thus what is called "tall" is dependent on what's called "short." The *Sun Tzu* is permeated with awareness of this interdependence and its usefulness in reaching one's objective. Thus it says in chapter 7 that we move the army by making the circuitous way into a direct way for ourselves and the direct circuitous for our enemy.

We manage this by identifying an action that is easy to accomplish, because it engenders no opposition, and effective, because it fundamentally rearranges the environment to our advantage. Thus in two examples from chapter 6: "To go one thousand li without fear, go through unpeopled ground," or "To attack and surely take it, attack where they do not defend."

This world is in flux. What is not defended today may well be defended tomorrow. If at the moment our army is full and fleet, its soldiers will be hungry tomorrow, and in a swamp they will be slow. So what our army is, what it can or cannot do, is not fixed, is not its unchanging essence. Rather it is dependent on the conditions in which our troops will be put. We are not "objects"; we're in a process of trajectory through space and time, always reacting with others. The only constancy lies in the characteristics of a particular set of things, such as that our army will get hungry every day, or "When soldiers are near, things sell dearly. When things sell dearly, wealth is exhausted." These are patterns that can be recognized as they play themselves out through time.

As we seek to discern such patterns or clusters of events, it's crucial to note the tendency things have, their natural propensities. Some of these are simple: water always flows down, and most people do not want to die. But being complex human beings, soldiers have a vast repertory of possible reactions, and the world itself is endlessly complex. This is not more true for Sun Tzu's army than for our own, but the language of the *Sun Tzu*, coming out of ancient China, is already geared to account for these aspects of the world. The ever-changing nature of things doesn't undercut its sense of reality or its logic, nor is it a threat to its worldview. On the contrary, these things are central to it.

The *Sun Tzu* provides multiple examples of these tendencies, patterns or clusters of events, teaching us to recognize them everywhere around us. To do so effectively, we must learn to work with shih.

Shih

Our world is cohesive. But we can mark off temporary and shifting patterns within it, each of which possesses momentary advantages of a certain kind. The squirrel on the horse is an example of this: he can safely cross the stream. This complex idea is represented by a single Chinese word, *shih*. (It is pronounced "shir," almost without a vowel.)[2]

The original meaning of *shih* was the power of the ruler—his control over others, his ability to affect them from a distance. By the time of the *Sun Tzu*, people had begun to recognize that this power did not rest in the ruler's person but in his position. As an early text notes:

> The Rearing Serpent sports in the mists,
> The Flying Dragon rides on the clouds.
> But when the clouds are gone and the mists have cleared,
> They are no different from earthworms.[3]

Before the time of the *Sun Tzu*, qualifications for power and authority included physical strength, esteemed ancestry and moral virtue. How is it that the contemporary ruler, who might have none of those qualities, nonetheless controlled those who did? The answer is that his authority, or shih, derives from his position on the throne. Being in that right place enormously magnifies his influence.

That position is not something he creates by himself. It requires the whole of the state apparatus, the participation of courtiers, bureaucrats and military men. Thus the ruler is powerful because he is at the head of a complex set of relationships. By contrast, personal strength, morality and ability are qualities that belong only to an individual. They are ineffective unless conjoined with larger patterns of influence.

Shih, then, is a function of the relationship among things. Its power rests in a particular conformation—the earthworm riding the wind high in the clouds, the ruler ordering his mechanisms of state. It depends on things arranged to connect with other things.

Now, such things change. When they do, their configuration alters as well. Then the power of their particular shih is no longer available. Thus the *Sun Tzu* remarks that the military has no fixed shih or lasting form (chapter 6). Without the clouds the dragon is just a worm, the ruler an ordinary man. But such changes are not random. One can determine whether tomorrow will bring winds and clouds to support the dragon. And an effective strategist knows when the tide will go out, allowing his troops to cross the estuary.

It may be simplest to take advantage of naturally occurring shih, but it's also wise to learn the small alterations you can make to the environment so that it works suddenly in your favor. The skillful strategist knows how to block the river so that the tide will not come back in until his enemy's troops are crossing the empty riverbed, whereupon he breaks the dam. Shih, in other words, can be cultivated. This may entail accumulation of energy or power bit by bit, the way water builds up behind a dam.

Shih, then, is like looking at a chessboard: the effectiveness of a position is read in terms of the relative power of certain pieces, the strength of their formation, their relationship to the opponent and also their potential to turn into something else. To these we might add the particular psychological disposition of our opponent. All are aspects of shih. They are analytically distinguishable, but a chess player sees all of them at once.

The world is more complex than three- or even five-dimensional chess. It includes food, shelter, rest, matériel—everything with which this discussion began. And there's a further crucial notion, which is timing: the right moment to step in, to take the shot, to release the accumulated energy. In the *Sun Tzu* this moment is called the *node*. It refers to the bumpy boundary between segments of bamboo, the little collar that separates each section from the next. It is very small.

Let's look, then, at how the *Sun Tzu* introduces these facets of shih. Each of the following passages from chapter 5 emphasizes a different aspect, though of course all aspects are subtly present. First is power-in-motion:

> The rush of water, to the point of tossing rocks
> about. This is shih.
> The strike of a hawk, at the killing snap. This is the
> node.

Water is soft, but here its massive rush tosses rocks about. This power comes from the intense movement of an otherwise harmless element. It is not evoked by changing the basic nature of water, only by amassing it and setting it in motion. The striking hawk, used here to characterize the node, also recalls the power of shih, suggesting how closely intertwined the two ideas are.

The second example emphasizes shape:

> Therefore, one skilled at battle—
> His shih is steep.
> His node is short.

The word *steep* could also be translated as "the ravine." Here the emphasis is on configuration, that shaping through which something draws on one of its latent qualities to manifest in quite another guise. The node is also made explicitly short.

The third example stresses the accumulation aspect:

> Shih is like drawing the crossbow.
> The node is like pulling the trigger.

The crossbow is a device for storing one's strength in the form of potential energy. Pulling the trigger sends off the bolt, releasing it all at once. This is shih in action. Power is accumulated, then focused perfectly. It's not that the bolt possesses power nor that it "borrows" the power of the bow. Power happens only when *all* the elements are present. It does not have a single source within the configuration nor anywhere outside it. At the right moment, or node, the bolt is released, striking a distant enemy.

All these aspects of shih come together in this example, also from chapter 5:

> One who uses shih sets people to battle as if rolling
>   trees and rocks.
> As for the nature of trees and rocks—
>   When still, they are at rest.
>   When agitated, they move.
>   When square, they stop.
>   When round, they go.
> Thus the shih of one skilled at setting people to
>   battle is like rolling round rocks from a
>   mountain one thousand jen high.

Here is power-in-movement, the right configuration and the release of potential energy. Rocks have varying natures and tendencies. The square ones don't roll, but the round, when properly agitated, surely will. Good shih lets us roll round rocks from a mountain a mile high. There is no need to push the rocks uphill nor to strike the corners off the square ones. Use the square to build fortifications, and roll the round ones down on the enemy. The right configuration makes this power naturally available.

With shih it is not necessary to alter the nature of things—as if water could only be a weapon if frozen into blocks of ice, or troops had to be courageous. Good shih will turn anyone into an effective soldier. The text says we need not rely on the particular qualities people possess:

> And so one skilled at battle
> Seeks it in shih and does not demand it of people.

Thus one can dispense with people and employ
shih. [Chapter 5]

This is the great, impersonal power of the world to which shih
points us.

Learning Shih

Shih exists only moment to moment. But one can learn to recognize it and thereby act effectively. Although in some other military traditions, victory may be attributed to the commander's
will, a perfect battle plan or overwhelming weight of numbers,
in the *Sun Tzu* it comes from mastery of shih. Like the squirrel
crossing the stream, we need to measure the situation carefully,
assess whether the water is placid or rushed, and if rushed,
whether we are strong enough to cross. We also need the ability
to assess it for its potential shih, as someone with a good eye
knows which way water will flow through a range of hills, just
from seeing the form of a valley and its surrounding spurs and
ridges. Then we can determine where to place a dam in this land-
scape—seeing the simple and easy thing that changes the whole
configuration.

The *Sun Tzu* teaches us shih in many ways. Three are especially important. The first uses a short phrase to summarize a complex argument. We have already seen several examples of this:
"And so one skilled at battle seeks it in shih and does not demand
it of people." The text also uses this mode to teach us the larger
view:

Taking a state whole is superior.
Destroying it is inferior to this.

That passage continues with a generalization and then a set of
further principles:

Therefore, one hundred victories in one hundred
    battles is not the most skillful.
Subduing the other's military without battle is the
    most skillful.

And so the superior military cuts down strategy.
Its inferior cuts down alliances.
Its inferior cuts down the military.
The worst attacks walled cities. [Chapter 3]

These statements derive from a perspective that takes whole. If
we didn't know them from within that larger view, we'd think of
them as no more than tangentially related individual insights.

Second, the text teaches by metaphor and image: "The rush of
water, to the point of tossing rocks about. This is shih." Shih is
"like drawing the crossbow," "like rolling round rocks from a
mountain one thousand jen high." These images remain with us,
shaping our thought in ways we may not consciously recognize.
Their power cannot be reproduced in linear prose.

The third way of teaching shih is simply showing examples of
it. Thus the text says things like, "In crossing mountains, hold to
the valleys," or "In crossing water, one must distance oneself from
it" (chapter 9). We could read these initially as simple admoni-
tions—in situation A do R. They are good advice from the front
lines, simple and clean. More fundamentally, however, they
express the world in terms of relationships. They describe what a
circumstance looks like if we assume the view and what we would
automatically do in response. Instead of enunciating these as
principles, the text instantiates them—gives us examples of them
concretely embedded.

Much of chapters 8 to 11 consists of this kind of information.
Sometimes it is presented as typologies of action. The nine
grounds, for example, are nine types of terrain; a certain pattern
of activity is appropriate to each. Much of the content seems
rather obvious. These may in fact be the earliest strata of the text,

with data arranged into groups of five or nine to facilitate memorization. But they are no less profound than the more conceptually complex chapters at the start of the book, for they derive from and express the same view.

And they teach shih just as surely, steeping us in the examples until we intuit the relational view, entirely bypassing the concept-based training of other chapters. This is the way one learns Aikido or karate, working with the *kata*, or form-sequences, repeating them until they are second nature, or first nature. It's also the way an oral tradition sustains a culture. Its maxims slip in under our consciousness, and their wisdom enters the mind-stream. This approach becomes problematic only when we try to reproduce the behavior of the maxims, instead of using them to trigger insight for the present circumstance.

Through these forms of training, we come to experience the world differently. All the time the nature of things is being pointed out to us. From this we learn to act spontaneously and appropriately in any new situation.

Knowing Tao

There is a final aspect of shih we must explore. To do so requires an act of imagination. We normally consider the world to be made up of solid things. Rocks are a perfect example—in particular, the round rocks the *Sun Tzu* suggests we might roll down a mountain one thousand jen high. But their solidity is only relative. Certainly they are harder, more condensed than human flesh, and human flesh is in turn harder or more concentrated than the air through which we move. But we could consider all of them on a single continuum.

Furthermore, each of these—rocks, people, air—assumes its shape only temporarily, appearing for longer or shorter times. These forms constantly interact with one another. This is true not only of active agents like people but also of immobile elements such as cliff faces. These are in relationship with the elements around them in that they make homes for birds and have steep canyon walls that keep soldiers from readily ascending.

Like any part of the world we might provisionally mark off, that canyon has boundaries, and people and things will move through it in a patterned way. We can take advantage of that flow, in some instances riding its energy. A text contemporaneous with the *Sun Tzu* says that the woolly seeds of the aster "encounter a whirlwind and voyage a thousand miles. They mount the shih of the wind."[4] Thus, if properly situated, even the smallest object can achieve something remarkable. Alternatively we can control the movement of forces, sending cascades of water through the ravine to sweep an enemy away. Our opponents are positioned where they become an obstacle to this flow and must expend considerable resources resisting it. The world, then, consists not of solid things but of flows of forces or movements of energy or shifting configurations of shih. These are Tao.

The chief impediment to knowing Tao is fixation. Instead of being the water cascading through the ravine, we are our own enemy, impeding its flow. We hold to a diminished view, a small part within the larger movement, rather than moving fluidly through it. We can become fixated in many ways. One is a matter of habit, ancient patterns of thought, like rivulets in the sand through which our thoughts always run. Good habits can be as limiting as bad. The text lists several qualities of the general that in the right circumstances are virtues. Here, held to an extreme, they become self-destructive:

> Resolved to die, one can be killed.
> Resolved to live, one can be captured.
> Quick to anger, one can be goaded.
> Pure and honest, one can be shamed.
> Loving the people, one can be aggravated.
> [Chapter 8]

These virtues have become a huge drag upon the general's movement. Indeed, *any* fixed quality is an impediment.

Another obstacle is our own projections. These prevent us from learning anything we don't already know. We never see the enemy because we can't even see ourselves clearly. Thus our world, which arises fresh and new at every moment, turns into something stiffly familiar.

What motivates those projections? Fixation at a deeper level, holding on to a smaller view. From the perspective of Tao, this small view is always under siege. It's like a rock in a roaring stream: it holds firm a while—a few moments or maybe several centuries—then it is swept away. Recognizing this vulnerability, we may move to shore it up, defending it against the dizzying perspective of the large.

But if we take that large view, if we become the stream as well as the rock, if we see the rock itself as energy, not fixation, then we open to a bigger mind, beyond petty concerns, beyond self-importance. Thus the text says:

> He advances yet does not seek fame.
> He retreats yet does not avoid blame.
> He seeks only to preserve the people,
> And his advantage accords with that of the ruler.
> He is the treasure of the state. [Chapter 10]

In this conviction we need not worry that reasons of self may be distorting our judgment. If we see that a battle cannot be won, we need not fight it, even if commanded to do so.

> And so when according to the Tao of battle there is
>   certain victory and the ruler says do not do
>   battle, one can certainly do battle.

> When according to the Tao of battle there is no
>   victory and the ruler says one must do battle,
>   one can not do battle. [Chapter 10]

Knowing Tao is even larger than obedience to the sovereign. It requires a different way of using the mind. This is evident in a passage that talks about three ways of using form. Here "form" is the particular shape we give to things, and forming is the particular shaping we do to make things happen.

> Rely on form to bring about victory over the
>   multitude,
> And the multitude cannot understand.
> The elite all know the form by which I am
>   victorious,
> But no one knows how I determine the form of
>   victory.
> Do not repeat the means of victory,
> But respond to form from the inexhaustible.
>   [Chapter 6]

Ordinary people see the victory, but they cannot discern the form of it. They only know things that are subject to ready calculations—the physical elements of warfare, logistics, that which can be counted. In the second kind of knowing, people are able to discern the forms we used. They already know all the elements of strategy—reversals, abstract kinds of calculation, how to set the few against the many. But it is only in retrospect that they recognize the particular way we have put all these together to come to victory. The third kind of knowing is inaccessible even to the elite. It is profoundly generative—from within it one is able to create new forms. This is responding to form from the inexhaustible, from something truly huge, from Tao.

Tao is many things. One is a special kind of chaos—chaos in the original Greek sense of a whole whose parts are not individually discernible. It is the order constituted by the totality of these multiple, changing relationships. But Tao is also the way things work, the way they move, the patterns they make in time as well as space.

How do we know Tao? In the same way that we know ordinary things such as turning off the stove when the teakettle has boiled. Both are apprehended effortlessly through immediate awareness of the situation. We also know Tao from learning shih. In that process we began by examining all the elements of our world and then seeing how they interacted, each with the other. Seeing the world as shih, noticing the fleeting configurations of things, we can discern appropriate action. We can respond to things from Tao, creating forms, the temporary patterns that cause things to happen.

Though Tao may seem like a system, a whole wherein all chaotic forces are unified, in fact there is no Tao other than this movement. Thus, as we might expect from the *Sun Tzu*, the culmination of this practice of form points beyond itself:

> The ultimate in giving form to the military is to
> arrive at formlessness.
> When one is formless, deep spies cannot catch a
> glimpse and the wise cannot strategize.
> [Chapter 6]

The corollary of formlessness is utter flexibility. This passage addresses the way that both armies and water assume their form:

> Now the form of the military is like water.
> Water in its movement avoids the high and hastens
> to the low.
> The military in its victory avoids the solid and
> strikes the empty.
> Thus water determines its movement in accordance
> with the earth.
> The military determines victory in accordance with
> the enemy.
> The military is without fixed shih and without
> lasting form.

> To be able to transform with the enemy is what is
> meant by "spiritlike." [Chapter 6]

Water's Tao is to flow downward. That's both what it is and what it does. The military is similar. Neither has a necessary shape, form, essence, self nor state of mind. They simply respond to the conditions around them.

"To be able to transform with the enemy is what is meant by 'spiritlike.'" Spirits are without substance, unfathomable. Again:

> Subtle! Subtle!
> To the point of formlessness.
> Spiritlike! Spiritlike!
> To the point of soundlessness.
> Thus one can be the enemy's fate star. [Chapter 6]

This is not a matter of belief in strange forces. Rather, it is about how things work. It is also about our human capacity to work with the world—to see, hear and know it and to find appropriate action there.

The Sage Commander

THE SUN TZU IS ADDRESSED TO THE GENERAL, THE PERSON WHO wields power in the midst of contention and conflict. He is the sage commander, an extraordinary example of human skill and wisdom. He speaks with authority, is effective, resourceful, in tune with larger patterns. He commands the battlefield. In this essay, from a consideration of his individual qualities and their interconnectedness, we begin to build an image of this wisdom as it is embodied in a human being. The text hints at this portrait but never completes it for us. We first describe his being, then show how his qualities manifest in a number of ways, including daring and deception.

This description is not based on a historical figure of ancient China. Instead we seek to personify an idealized wisdom, making what might otherwise seem distant and unreachable relevant to our everyday life. Doing so enables us to identify genuine examples of people who manifest this wisdom and can transmit it to others. Upon closer examination we can see some element in each of his qualities and actions that reflects our own experience in situations of conflict.

In this way a semimythical person becomes more human and immediate. We sense the possibility of a model we might emulate and a discipline we can actually practice. Just like the sayings in the text that change our way of thinking with a few words, the image of the sage commander can reshape our actions during times of great challenge. This shows us taking whole, how to conquer without fighting.

The Military

In order to fully appreciate the role of the sage commander, we must first establish what we mean by the military. Most generally the military is an application of force, and its most common example is the army. Force is the exercise of strength, present in almost all physical and mental acts. The military, then, is an intensification of this common human activity.

Force is neutral. It becomes mixed with aggression, however, when one takes a smaller view, insisting that others conform to one's demands. Aggression brings devastation to all parties, including those who employ it:

> If the general is not victorious over his anger and
> sets them swarming like ants,
> One-third of the officers and soldiers are killed and
> the walled city not uprooted—
> This is the calamity of attack. [Chapter 3]

The military expresses this force, which it uses to protect the integrity of the state. By state the *Sun Tzu* most obviously means a political body. But state may also refer to any entity that represents the larger reference point. It could be a household, clan, culture or society. Alternatively it could be one's own mind. By protection we mean maintaining boundaries. These ensure the integrity of the whole, allowing life to flourish within them and assuring the proper exchange between what is inside and outside. Protection means respecting and guaranteeing their security, either through warding off or through extending outward—

through defending or conquering. It also includes ensuring the welfare of whatever the state relies on for its well-being.

This need for protection is a fundamental aspect of dualistic existence. That is, friction or opposition will occur in any situation in which there is an "inner" and an "outer," a separation into our side and the other side. This friction may be so mild and irrelevant as to be hardly noticeable. It could be a creative force. It is not necessarily negative or destructive. Performing any physical or mental work means overcoming the resistance that this opposition presents. In war that friction becomes extreme, difficult and all-consuming. The military exists to work in such situations.

In addition to representing the principle of protection, the military is the means by which a society focuses its resources to deal with times of crisis and profound change. These crises may be natural disasters, when the enemy is flood or famine. They may be the human disaster of war. Or they may be any occasion in which our state of mind is overwhelmed with confusion. Such situations demand hard choices about creation and destruction, life and death. Here the military acts as a container within which the society or individual can reestablish its integrity in the face of monumental threat. The military that takes whole preserves life.

The *Sun Tzu* addresses all these principles of the military. The text assumes that conflict arises naturally and is unavoidable, and that protection is a normal function the military serves. It also speaks of how to respond to chaos and change at the deepest levels. And in all cases the *Sun Tzu* shows us taking whole—moving beyond a habitual aggressive response toward conflict and discovering the possibility of victory. As the text says,

> One hundred victories in one hundred battles is not
> the most skillful.
> Subduing the other's military without battle is the
> most skillful. [Chapter 3]

A contemplative reading of the text serves to bring out this wisdom most fully. In the most fundamental sense, to contemplate means to create a protected space for observation. Just as tending a garden makes room to observe and care for the seeds you have planted, a contemplative approach provides room in your mind to see things in a simple and ordinary way. We are not speaking of contemplating any specific thing but simply creating openness for the consideration of whatever arises.

A well-known Zen story tells of a learned visitor to a monastery. He comes ostensibly to inquire about Zen but ends up lecturing the master on Buddhist theory and doctrine. The master listens politely and pours tea. Like his guest, he goes on and on, still pouring after the bowl is full and tea is running over the lip and across the tabletop. Thus he makes the point that the visitor's mind is too full to learn anything new.

Contemplation is an ordinary state of mind that all human beings experience. It consists most basically of openness and attention. We notice it when we are struck by a moment of beauty: the half-moon shining brightly through scattered clouds, the penetrating blue sky on a cold winter morning. Contemplative mind is the unformed, creative source that is tapped in the performing and plastic arts and is present in what athletes call "the zone." It is cultivated in any mind or body discipline that requires us to be fully present. This quality of mind is as much the wellspring of the military commander who sees the wholeness of the chaotic battlefield as of the potter who catches the unique form arising from the spinning lump of clay.

Contemplation fosters a direct experience of things rather than relying on theory alone. For the reader of the *Sun Tzu*, it creates a space where the sloganlike lines of the text can mix with the basic awareness and intelligence of his or her mind. This opens a dialogue between the text and the reader that continually reveals new meaning as the reader's understanding deepens.

But the fruition of a contemplative approach lies not in reading or recalling but in seeing the potential of whatever arises in the moment. This is how the sage commander "responds from the inexhaustible," the ultimate resourcefulness, and finds the way to the victories that "cannot be known in advance." It is how the reader becomes a member of this wisdom lineage.

Being

For the *Sun Tzu*, the key to skillful action is in knowing those things that make up the environment and then arranging them so that their power becomes available. The text calls this power *shih*. Working with shih begins with the way things are. It is not necessary to change the nature of things in order to come to victory.

The sage commander starts with himself. Thus his first question is not what to do but how to be. Simply being oneself brings about a power often lost in the rush to be something else. A rock is just a rock and a tree just a tree. But the text tells us:

> As for the nature of trees and rocks—
> When still, they are at rest.
> When agitated, they move.
> When square, they stop.
> When round, they go.
> Thus the shih of one skilled at setting people to
> battle is like rolling round rocks from a
> mountain one thousand jen high. [Chapter 5]

The torrent these things become as they roll down the mountainside is unstoppable.

Because the sage commander has settled into being who he is, he is no longer constantly comparing himself to others. He is not embarrassed and doesn't need to pretend to be more than he is. There is no gap between his words and his action. Thus he acts from his own ground of strength. Since his mind is not distracted, he can catch the opportunities that arise from each circumstance.

The sage commander is genuine because he appreciates himself as he is. This gives rise to gentleness, whereby he can allow things to be as they are rather than forcing them to be a certain way. This kindness is not based on the logic of ethics, nor do his actions necessarily conform to conventional standards of behavior.

Knowing how to be means that the sage commander doesn't hover above the ground or perch upon his seat but sits like a mountain, of the nature of the earth. Being who he is, he is a compass point by which others can obtain their bearings, so that they too can relax into who they are. This resolves the ground of any situation, sorting out confusion before it arises. Simply by being who he is, holding his seat, he has already accomplished much of his goal.

Since his activity radiates a quality of completeness, his actions display a deep conviction. This engenders trust, so others believe in what he does and says. Thus he leads the people and ensures the welfare of the state.

> Now the general is the safeguard of the state.
> If the safeguard is complete, the state is surely
>   strong.
> If the safeguard is flawed, the state is surely weak.
>   [Chapter 3]

When the sage commander leads the troops into battle, they must follow without hesitation. He works hard to earn this loyalty by knowing and caring for his soldiers. With natural inquisitiveness about how people function, the sage commander connects to his troops in an intimate and personal way.

> And so one skilled at employing the military takes
>   them by the hand as if leading a single person.
> They cannot hold back. [Chapter 11]

Every circumstance is an opportunity for the sage commander to cultivate this relationship, and every exchange can deepen his connection with his troops. Working in the trenches alongside the troops, the sage commander experiences their situation firsthand.

Loyalty is above all based on appreciation. It develops when people appreciate what they are involved in and when appreciation is expressed for them. The sage commander earns the loyalty of the troops by first genuinely expressing loyalty to them in even the smallest gestures. He doesn't miss the opportunity to win someone's trust and never gives up on anyone. In this way he creates a unified entity where before there were many individuals and gains a military that follows him through extreme conditions and conflict.

> He looks upon the troops as his children.
> Thus they can venture into deep river valleys
> with him.
> He looks upon the troops as his beloved sons.
> Thus they can die together with him.
> [Chapter 10]

His natural inquisitiveness manifests as respect for the intelligence of his troops. Even negativity is not an obstacle, since he responds to the intelligence expressed within it. Thus mutual respect strengthens the bond between the sage commander and his troops.

The bonds forged by intimate contact and mutual respect provide the ground for the military's hard training and difficult tasks. Constant socialization and reinforcement of values are necessary to build cohesiveness within the military. But it is through this kind of effort that these bonds can develop into a fierce loyalty.

The sage commander creates a uniform military out of an assembly of people through exertion and discipline. Here exertion is an even, continuous process. It goes beyond the alternation of off-duty and on-duty, thus avoiding the cycle of exertion, collapse and renewal.

And so one who knows the military
Acts and is not confused,
Initiates and is not exhausted.
    [Chapter 10]

Exertion is never giving up, but it isn't wearing oneself out. It's more like riding the wind than pushing a rock up a hill. The sage commander fosters an even exertion by developing a stronger personal connection to his goal.

Heaven is yin and yang, cold and hot, the order of
    the seasons.
Going with it, going against it—this is military
    victory. [Chapter 1]

The sage commander's exertion is "going with it," finding the natural energy and taking advantage of it. That can be as simple as not fighting uphill or not crossing a stream that is rushing from new rainfall. Or it could be as extraordinary as "hiding below the nine earths and moving above the nine heavens." The sage commander is not exhausted because instead of holding to a separate reality, he is able to "go with it."

This type of exertion comes out of a natural discipline. Discipline is commonly associated with applying an external regimen in order to improve behavior. Often it is a foreign element that never completely takes root. However, the sage commander develops a natural sense of discipline that is based on appreciating the world and going along with its natural patterns. When you appreciate your body, you eat things that are good for you, rather than forcing yourself onto a diet. Because he appreciates what is happening, he leans into the task with interest and energy rather than feeling that he is being dragged to a chore. This natural discipline is what brings him back to the task and reminds him of the larger perspective.

Working with Chaos

The sage commander is well prepared for battle. Genuine and authentic, he engenders a fundamental trust among his troops. Connected to the ground of things, he can respond with resourcefulness. His energy is even and continually replenished. His military is loyal and will follow him even into great danger.

But the ground of battle, and indeed all of life, is unpredictable, full of chaos and uncertainty. From an ordinary perspective, chaos is the disorder between the last discernible order and the future order that has not yet come. It is a dangerous and uncertain time, when things that seem solid and fixed fall apart.

Chaos is indeed a great challenge for the general. If he himself is chaotic, his ability to command the situation is seriously undermined.

> He is chaotic and unable to bring order. [Chapter 10]

And the outcome of his own confusion is a confused and ineffective military:

> The general is weak and not strict.
> His training and leadership are not clear.
> The officers and troops are inconstant.
> The formations of the military are jumbled.
> [Chapter 10]

The sage commander, however, always takes the bigger view. While in the midst of confusion, he sees how chaos forms its own particular order. Though the course of a hurricane along the coast is unpredictable, it is part of a weather pattern that is intelligible.

> Chaos is born from order.
> Cowardice is born from bravery.
> Weakness is born from strength. [Chapter 5]

Chaos and order are two aspects of the same thing. Together they constitute the totality of our experience, the good and bad, the confusion and clarity—how it is all interconnected and constantly shifting. From the smaller perspective, we experience these as opposed. But in order to take whole, the sage commander must work with this totality. He resides in the fundamental orderliness of the chaos, and thus for him,

> The fight is chaotic yet one is not subject to chaos.
> [Chapter 5]

Although chaos is generally a difficult and uncomfortable time, it is also dynamic, a time of great openness and creativity. The sage commander develops an appreciation for its potent quality. Since he holds no fixed position, chaos is not a threat. He is not undermined by uncertainty. Rather than giving in to the impulse to control chaos when it arises, the sage commander rests in the chaos and allows it to resolve itself.

This trust resembles conventional patience, in that the sage commander refrains from action. Yet rather than an act of forbearance, it is a matter of letting things happen in their own time. It is a withdrawing from the smaller skirmishes to allow a greater victory to ripen.

> When it has rained upstream, the stream's flow
> intensifies.
> Stop fording. Wait for it to calm. [Chapter 9]

Chaos then becomes a powerful time for the sage commander to take effective action. He can use it as an ally, particularly against a highly solidified position. Chaos can undermine that situation, unraveling it rather than forcing a confrontation. Trying to overpower solidity by building up greater solidity merely triggers the cycle of escalation.

Since the sage commander appreciates and accommodates

chaos, he sees more clearly what is taking place within it. Thus he knows how shih will develop and can catch the moment when one small gesture will be more decisive than a tremendous effort applied at the wrong time or place.

Being prepared and awaiting the unprepared is
victory. [Chapter 3]

Allowing a chaotic situation to develop demands courage, for it often means that in the short term things will get worse rather than better. There is always the chance that something of value will be harmed. But in the interplay of chaos and order, things don't always resolve themselves in a linear manner, so they must be allowed to run their course. Achieving a fundamental, long-term solution is more important than resolving immediate irritation and discomfort. So he allows the situation to develop and with patience finds the right moment to make the critical impact.

Faced with chaos or conflict, the sage commander looks first to the largest reference point. No matter what ground he has been given, he always thinks bigger. Loosening his gaze on the immediate and short term, suspending his habitual view, he looks to the space around things.

While maintaining a steady gaze on the larger goal of victory, the sage commander allows lesser objectives to change and develop naturally. These smaller goals are often woven closely together and in competition with one another. Yet even as they shift position and change shape, they can still support the larger goal. He is careful not to fixate on a particular way they might manifest and thereby avoids insignificant skirmishes. While remaining intimately in touch with even the smallest detail, the sage commander remains open to the larger pattern.

The best illustration of this is in how he works with problems. A problem usually arises when one holds to a view that has become too small and inflexible. Addressing a problem as it is presented often reinforces the fixation that initially gave rise to it.

The sage commander focuses on the bigger perspective that holds the key to both the problem and the solution. There he can catch the possibilities that are hidden from others and attain the victory they cannot see.

> In seeing victory, not going beyond what everyone
> knows is not skilled.
> Victory in battle that all-under-heaven calls skilled
> is not skilled. [Chapter 4]

The Sage Commander in the World

The *Sun Tzu* recognizes that conflict is painful and destructive and that responding to it effectively can require tough measures and a strong hand. It deals with the totality of conflict. This is particularly necessary for the sage commander, since he seeks to take the enemy whole.

For all that the text tells us about the general's good qualities—"knowledge, trustworthiness, courage and strictness"—he is clearly not a conventional model citizen. He is willing to do whatever is required to bring about victory, including many things that might not normally be considered acceptable acts for a sage. He uses spies, deceives and throws his troops into death ground. He holds to no standards of behavior save what will bring the genuine victory of taking whole. He is not what others expect, not where others look and not predictable in any way.

The sage commander acts without care for others' opinions of his methods or his own reputation. Always keeping victory in the forefront, he is not restricted to reasonability and negotiation but will use whatever motivates people in order to create favorable shih.

> Therefore—
> Do not contend for allies in all-under-heaven.
> Do not cultivate balance in all-under-heaven.

Trust in self-interest.
Spread one's awesomeness over the enemy.
Thus his state can be seized and his walled cities
can be made to submit. [Chapter 11]

We have seen the sage commander looking upon the troops as his children, thereby creating a loyal army that will follow him into battle (chapter 10). But the sage commander does not hesitate to substitute harm for kindness if necessary to produce the same effect:

Bind them with deeds. Do not command them with
words.
Bind them with harm. Do not command them with
advantage. [Chapter 11]

In fact, one cannot be sure that any activity is outside the sage commander's arsenal of behavior when victory is at stake. He determines all his actions in relation to the objective of taking whole. He might rule out devastation of the enemy on the battlefield, as it would defeat that larger objective. But this doesn't eliminate other extreme measures. As the text tells us, he may set fire to people (chapter 12) and even kill the enemy general if necessary to attain victory without bringing his or the enemy's troops into the danger of full battle:

And so conducting the affairs of the military
Lies in carefully discerning the enemy's purpose.
Concentrate strength in one direction.
Go one thousand li and kill his general. [Chapter 11]

What are the boundaries of the sage commander's daring and outrageous actions? What, if anything, distinguishes them from the brutal, self-centered activity of the tyrant? In doing whatever is necessary to attain victory, the sage commander has the courage to bring others to the larger perspective that they cannot initially see. His actions are not limited and self-centered because they encompass the views of both his enemies and his allies. The sage commander seeks a resolution to conflict that takes whole. As the text says,

> He seeks only to preserve the people. [Chapter 10]

The source of all this skillful action is knowledge, which the text tells us is the first quality of the sage commander. Knowing begins with the myriad details that make up his world. Whose officers are trained? What is the form of the mountains and forests? What are the strategies of the feudal lords? His knowledge of such details must be clear, accurate and reliable. But the text quickly emphasizes that this is about more than information.

> And so in the military—
> Knowing the other and knowing oneself,
> In one hundred battles no danger.
> Not knowing the other and knowing oneself,
> One victory for one loss.
> Not knowing the other and not knowing
> oneself,
> In every battle certain defeat. [Chapter 3]

For the sage commander, knowing oneself comes back to the quality of being simply and genuinely who one is. From this basic orientation, he develops a natural appreciation of his environment. This relaxes the struggle to grasp knowledge as something external, and the world opens up. Knowing isn't so much hard work and accumulation as it is appreciating and making a personal connection to the world. The sage commander's knowing becomes an unbiased perception, in which things are no longer regarded as either for one or against one but are seen with a dispassionate judgment.

Always keeping the larger perspective foremost in mind, the sage commander clearly sees both the details of the world and the environment in which these details occur. Holding both of these in his mind at the same time, he begins to see the patterns that the details form. Perceiving their interconnectedness, he knows the arcs through which they may progress. Yet there is no certainty about how any single thing will turn out. This is how the sage commander begins to read the world and see the Tao of things.

From knowing the pattern of things, the sage commander is able to penetrate beneath the surface of phenomena until he reaches the seed or kernel. The seed contains all the qualities of a thing but does not determine exactly how each quality will manifest. A poppy seed will predictably produce a poppy, but each poppy will be unique. The sage commander who knows the world in this way is able to work with the whole from any of the parts. From a person's smile, he can tell his intent. In his tone of voice, he can read the whole of his message. This is both ordinary and very powerful. It is the most profound knowing of all.

> And so it is said—
> Know the other and know oneself,
> Then victory is not in danger.
> Know earth and know heaven,
> Then victory can be complete. [Chapter 10]

Knowing heaven and earth at every level of manifestation— the terrain and the weather, the obstacles and the possibilities, the details and the bigger perspective—allows the sage commander's knowledge to begin at one small point and expand to the whole. In this way he is able to get to the heart of victory in battle. Knowing gives rise to skillful actions that allow him to attain the ultimate victory of taking whole. He achieves victories that others cannot see, victories that are total and inexhaustible.

Thus it is said, "Victory can be known. It cannot be made." [Chapter 4]

From knowing the world in this way, the sage commander can begin to shape the appearance of the details and the patterns to bring about victory. This is using deception. Deception is controlling what others see and, by doing so, shaping the conclusions that they draw. It usually has a strong negative connotation, as in manipulation for the purpose of fulfilling self-centered objectives. When it separates people from their own hopes and goals, it leaves them feeling duped or betrayed.

For the sage commander, however, deception is a means of bringing others around to a larger view, one that includes their own objectives, without going to battle. The sage commander moves the enemy where he wants them to be, both figuratively and literally, by having them see what he wants them to see. If his deception has a limited objective, it is not to fulfill a goal that excludes others but to be a stepping-stone to the larger victory.

The sage commander sees others' perceptions and projections clearly and from that knows what they will see. He shapes the ground to deceive them, with actions that fit, like glove on hand, the enemy's own mind and action.

To be able to transform with the enemy is what is meant by "spiritlike." [Chapter 6]

The sage commander holds no fixed position or identity. Thus he is free to be whatever he needs to be to achieve victory. If he is fully engaged in whatever form he takes, then his manifestation is genuine.

The sage commander uses deception to keep others from knowing his methods and his intentions. He can make himself totally ungraspable and beyond the reach of the enemy's intelligence. Often he appears the direct opposite of his actual condition:

Thus when able, manifest inability.
When active, manifest inactivity.
When near, manifest as far.
When far, manifest as near. [Chapter 1]

Knowing is the basis for the general's action in the world. By preventing the enemy from accurately knowing him, the sage commander's skillful deception renders the enemy action ineffective and without a target.

Thus with one skilled at attack, the enemy does not
know where to defend.
With one skilled at defense, the enemy does not
know where to attack. [Chapter 6]

Deception can be as simple for the sage commander as confirming the projections that others present. In this case he takes no action but merely allows the projection to be, without embarrassment or resistance. Since the sage commander does not hold to a fixed position, the projection does not capture him and is not a threat. By resisting, he might become mired in an irrelevant skirmish that leads away from victory. By allowing the enemy's projection to remain unquestioned, he relaxes their initiative while waiting for the shih to change in his favor.

The skillful sage commander can create a compelling new reality to replace the one to which the enemy holds. On a clear night in the country, many stars shine brightly in the sky. Yet when the sun rises, it is as if they no longer exist. The sage commander can shine a light on one part of the scene to focus the enemy's attention there, leaving other parts fully imperceptible.

The most powerful form of deception is to create the existence of that which does not exist in order to create the nonexistence of that which exists. Thus he can hide in front of people's eyes:

> If I do not wish to do battle, I mark a line on the
> earth to defend it, and the enemy cannot do
> battle with me.
> I misdirect him. [Chapter 6]

But since the sage commander doesn't hold to a fixed position, he also doesn't need to proclaim his victorious deception. Most deception goes unnoticed, and the greatest deception leaves no trace.

Victory

According to the *Sun Tzu*, victory arises only in the moment.

> These are the victories of the military lineage.
> They cannot be transmitted in advance. [Chapter 1]

How, then, does the sage commander find victory? Once again, this comes back to knowing—first himself and then the other—as the source of all skillful action. Relying on his own genuineness, he creates the ground for victory in his actions, environment, but most important, in his mind.

> Do not rely on their not coming.
> Rely on what we await them with.
> Do not rely on their not attacking.
> Rely on how we are unable to be attacked.
> [Chapter 8]

The sage commander is beyond the sway and manipulation of others. His preparation, then, is not so much focused on accumulating strength as on taking a position outside the reach of attack. His perspective prepares the ground of no defeat.

One skilled at battle takes a stand in the ground of
    no defeat
And so does not lose the enemy's defeat.
Therefore, the victorious military is first victorious
    and after that does battle.
The defeated military first does battle and after that
    seeks victory. [Chapter 4]

Thus he steps outside the possibility of attack altogether, remaining beyond grasp. If he cannot be found, the enemy has nothing against which to fight.

Of old those skilled at defense hid below the nine
    earths and moved above the nine heavens.
Thus they could preserve themselves and be all-
    victorious. [Chapter 4]

The sage commander moves beyond defeat by being victorious over his own aggression. He neither ignores nor indulges in it. Giving in to aggression is the root of the destructive process of warfare. It can be overwhelming and lead one to prevail by devastating the enemy. This makes one susceptible to defeat. As the text says, the general who is not victorious over his anger brings destruction to his own troops as well as to the enemy.

Aggression gives the enemy something against which to fight. This mires the general in battle. The sage commander responds to aggression by creating space, which relaxes the situation and paradoxically brings it more under his control. It's like controlling a bull by giving him a very large pasture.

Residing in victory, the sage commander creates both the ground for the enemy defeat to arise and the openness to catch it when it does. In this way he is victorious before the battle is fought.

The sage commander establishes a victorious situation by extending the ground of no defeat out into the world. He is able to accomplish this because he knows so intimately the forms of the ground, what they are made up of and how they work. Everything he does reiterates and supports this all-victorious perspective, generating wave after wave of consistent strategic activity, so that the victorious situation builds upon itself. The text refers to this as "spread[ing] one's awesomeness over the enemy" (chapter 11).

The sage commander's awesomeness is not static. It is open and sensitive to the ever-changing ground, so that it remains timely and refreshed.

> Rely on form to bring about victory over the
>   multitude,
> And the multitude cannot understand.
> The elite all know the form by which I am
>   victorious,
> But no one knows how I determine the form of
>   victory. [Chapter 6]

The sage commander forms the ground and brings others around to his victorious perspective. He forms himself as well as the environment and thus narrows the enemy options. He offers them the choices he wants them to have and leads them where he wants them to go. The sage commander attains victory when the enemy can see no other alternative and chooses what he has offered. He is all-victorious when they see that option as best for them and have no idea that they were directed there.

> One skilled at moving the enemy
>   Forms and the enemy must follow,
>   Offers and the enemy must take. [Chapter 5]

The text suggests various ways in which the sage commander may shape the ground. In general his activity is based on forming and transforming himself and the environment in relation to the enemy. He uses this to create advantage for himself. There is no single, fixed position or form that brings advantage. Instead advantage changes in each situation and is always relative to the enemy:

> Now the form of the military is like water.
> Water in its movement avoids the high and hastens
>   to the low.
> The military in its victory avoids the solid and
>   strikes the empty.
> Thus water determines its movement in accordance
>   with the earth.
> The military determines victory in accordance with
>   the enemy.
> The military is without fixed shih and without
>   lasting form.
>
> To be able to transform with the enemy is what is
>   meant by "spiritlike." [Chapter 6]

The Tao of the circuitous and the direct is one method the sage commander uses to shape the ground. When he can reach an objective faster than the enemy expects or turn a seeming weakness into strength, the enemy's ground is turned upside down. Their assessment of time and direction is proved wrong, undermining their confidence in their own perceptions. Similarly, drawing the enemy away from a direct path confuses them, upsets their plan and undermines their knowledge.

> Thus make their road circuitous
> And lure them with advantage.
> Setting out later than others and arriving sooner
> Is knowing the appraisals of circuitous and direct.
>   [Chapter 7]

And then,

> One who knows in advance the Tao of the
> circuitous and direct is victorious.
> This is the method of the army contending.
> [Chapter 7]

The sage commander also transforms in order to create an imbalance between himself and the enemy. When his weight and power far exceed the enemy's, it is creating a preponderance. This is not based merely on accumulation of resources. As the text tells us, "In the military more is not better" (chapter 9). Rather, the sage commander finds a position that is forceful and solid relative to the enemy and applies his strength where the enemy is weak and empty.

> How a military comes to prevail, like throwing a
> grindstone against an egg.
> It is the empty and the solid. [Chapter 5]

The ultimate in creating preponderance is shih, which is simultaneously the configuration of forces and the power inherent within them. The sage commander forms the ground to bring about favorable shih. As the text tells us, he doesn't change the nature of things, only their circumstances. Thus he gains their power. As the sage commander shapes the ground to create advantage, he waits for the node to arise and then swiftly acts. This is the critical moment when preponderance can be applied and victory assured.

> A victorious military is like weighing a
> hundredweight against a grain.
> A defeated military is like weighing a grain against
> a hundredweight.
> One who weighs victory sets the people to battle
> like releasing amassed water into a gorge one
> thousand jen deep. [Chapter 4]

By mastering these actions of forming and transforming, the sage commander shapes and prepares the ground for taking whole. In this complex and essentially uncontrollable world, the ultimate outcome of present actions is not predictable. Today's enemy may be a friend tomorrow. The sage commander seeks a victory that is ongoing. Taking whole allows him to preserve the possibilities—to keep every option open.

Taking whole means conquering the enemy in a way that keeps as much intact as possible—both your own resources and those of the enemy. Such a victory leaves something available to build upon, for both you and your former foe. Destruction leaves nothing, and its aftermath diverts valuable energy from the larger victory.

> One must take it whole when contending for all-
> under-heaven.
> Thus the military is not blunted and advantage can
> be whole. [Chapter 3]

Taking whole starts with defeating the enemy's strategy, both large and small. Strategy is the means by which all actions are coordinated and all resources allocated. The enemy's strategy makes their actions coherent and focused. Defeating that strategy unravels the enemy's cohesion and dissolves their alliances. Thus the sage commander renders the physical destruction of their forces unnecessary. He accomplishes this through the skillful use of forming and transforming the ground of battle. This is as much a matter of mind as it is of the physical conditions of warfare.

> And so the superior military cuts down strategy.
> Its inferior cuts down alliances.
> Its inferior cuts down the military.
> The worst attacks walled cities. [Chapter 3]

Swiftness rules when it comes to taking whole (chapter 11). It allows the sage commander's military to seize the moment when advantage arises. The sage commander's patience allows him to await that moment. When it comes, he can act with lightning swiftness. All in all, he gets to the heart of the matter as quickly as possible. He is not slowed by relating to what the enemy chooses to show but sees the purpose behind their actions, making quick work of a conflict that could otherwise be destructive for all.

The most profound method the sage commander employs to attain victory is the extraordinary and the orthodox. He engages the enemy with what they expect. This is the orthodox, that which is familiar and understandable, what the enemy can easily see. It confirms their projections. However, the sage commander conquers the enemy with what they never imagine. This is the extraordinary. It is not any particular action but simply what the enemy does not expect.

To do so, he works with the enemy's perception of the world. If the enemy believes the sage commander's position to be protected, they will not attack, regardless of whether that position is in fact undefended. More than anything, the sage commander must understand his enemy's processes of thought. Whatever the nature of someone's thinking, strong or weak, it forms a pattern. As such, it systematically includes and excludes. These are both its strengths and its limitations. If the sage commander can discern the enemy's pattern, he knows what is orthodox within it. Then, in response, the extraordinary is apparent to him:

> One skilled at giving rise to the extraordinary—
> As boundless as heaven and earth,
> As inexhaustible as the Yellow River and the
> ocean. [Chapter 5]

The patterns of his enemy's thought are obvious to the sage commander, the way a road map indicates where the next highway exit leads or a facial expression reveals so much about someone's intention. Part of this comes from familiarity with the world. However, it is less a matter of specific information than of his understanding of basic human existence. All these are still the orthodox. But he himself always thinks bigger, seeing beyond them into something the enemy cannot conceive. This doesn't require special equipment or techniques. It works with the ordinary things of the world and has a quality of everyday magic.

THE ALL-VICTORIOUS SAGE COMMANDER doesn't attain victory by bringing the enemy over to his side. Instead he creates a larger view that includes both sides. It is the ground from which all interests arise. But there is no promise of victory, no formula or guideline that will ultimately ensure that victory comes about. Nor is there is an absolute measure of victory. The sage commander can only refer back to his ground of basic genuineness.

Taking whole is victory over aggression. It arises in the unique moment of each circumstance. It preserves the possibilities. Victory is ongoing, a way of being rather than a final goal. It means embracing all aspects of the world. Trying to reject parts of it perpetuates the struggle, in oneself and in the world. Victory over war is victory over this aggression, a victory that includes the enemy and thus renders further conflict unnecessary.

Joining the Tradition

SOMETIME DURING THE FOURTH CENTURY BCE, THE SUN TZU emerged from the oral tradition and for the first time took on written form. It offered a radical response to fundamental issues facing the states of north China, matters, it said, "of death and life, survival or extinction." We believe the text is as significant today as it was then. But when we seek to understand a historical document as a living tradition, a special set of issues arises. Can we grasp this work on its own terms? Or do our concerns, coming from a twenty-first–century EuroAmerican perspective, distort the text rather than illuminate it?

These are fundamental questions about the uses of the past. An identical statement made in ancient China and present-day America may mean two very different things. How can we recognize this difference and then presume to overcome it? To determine this, we must first examine the context within which the *Sun Tzu* came into being, noting the questions its contemporaries sought to answer. We can then evaluate to what extent the text is tied to its origins, identifying as well the strategy by which it frees itself from them. We will discover a pair of paradoxical truths: the *Sun Tzu* is both intimately connected to the specific conditions of Warring States China and equally beyond the limitations of that time and place.

As we seek to continue the *Sun Tzu* tradition, what additional information does the form of the text provide? Does it welcome our participation? If so, how? What makes the tradition open to us now, and what must we do if we wish to join it? The answers lie in the way the *Sun Tzu* emerged from the oral tradition. That process was above all cumulative, not a single act. It remained open to additions even after a definitive fourth-century BCE editing. The integrity of the text, then, depends less on an unchanging set of words than on its underlying perspective, its view of taking whole. If we trace its words back until we learn to assume that view, then it is possible for us to join the tradition.

Finally, what is it about our world today that makes this possibility so compelling? Why do people everywhere read this book? Here we consider how developments of the last hundred years have led to an environment that understands the *Sun Tzu* as a living text. Thus each of these three aspects—its context, form and environment—shows how an authentic present tradition of the *Sun Tzu* can be established.

The Warring States Context

This investigation starts in 1045 BCE, when the Chou people conquered north China and established a dynasty that would last until 256 BCE. To rule an area the size of Western Europe, the Chou kings appointed seventy-some families as fief holders and garrison keepers, each bound by ties of blood or marriage to the throne. Gradually these fiefs became quasi-independent states, whose rivalries sometimes led to violence. The military ideals of that era were based on chivalric practices comparable to those of medieval Europe or Japan. Aristocrats fought their peers in chariots. Oaths of kings and nobles were sealed in blood, honor jealously defended. Military codes stipulated fair treatment of one's enemy, and loss on the battlefield did not yet entail the extinction of one's state.

As the kinship of rulers became attenuated, the frequency and severity of interstate battles increased. By the sixth century BCE, when Confucius lived, the political power of the Chou king was largely symbolic. In 453 BCE a major state was seized by its leading families and torn in three, initiating the period of the Warring States. A century later, as the *Sun Tzu* was assembled, chivalric patterns survived only in myth. Aristocratic chariots had given way to huge armies of peasant conscripts, who were driven onto the field, armed with crossbows and iron-tipped weapons. Cavalrymen adopted the trousers of the northern barbarians. Recurrent battles engulfed the populace in unprecedented acts of destruction far from home. Victors won a striking upward mobility, whereas the consequences of defeat were slavery, death and the eradication of one's ruling house. Of the multitude of early states, only seven major contenders survived. Then in 222 BCE the ruler of Ch'in overcame his remaining opponents and proclaimed himself First Emperor of China.

The Warring States brought enormous change to every aspect of Chinese society. Fighting destroyed the common morality as well as ancient fiefs. Scores of advisers flocked the feudal courts offering conflicting advice on the central question: "How does one establish order in all-under-heaven?" For the first time, written texts helped drive this development—administrative manuals, cosmic speculations, Confucian discourses on morality and ritual, utopian social projects. Their varied doctrines would become the foundation of Chinese political thought for the subsequent two thousand years.[1]

The security of his state was the heart of every sovereign's concern. The military was the chief means to attain this goal, both outside and within the realm. Military forms of organization were therefore increasingly applied in civil society. Rulers implemented strict legal codes, backed by sophisticated systems of mutual responsibility and reward and punishment.[2] Accompanying these were military texts that focused on strategy, tactics, organization, logistics, training and the general's relationship with the state. Many dozens of these must have been written, for some forty are mentioned in the imperial library catalog of the late first century BCE, and half a dozen still survive to this day.[3] Most renowned is the *Sun Tzu*.

This *Sun Tzu* differs from all contemporaneous texts. It has nothing of Confucian morality or ritual concerns about it. Though it seeks to create cohesive social units, it is not based on the administrators' reward-and-punishment system. Its style of thinking—reversal, polarities and spiritlike transformation—is closest to the Taoists, but it does not oppose the use of force. Other military texts offer highly specific technical advice on logistics and formations. But the *Sun Tzu* emphasizes knowledge as a means of attaining victory, and its principal weapon is the power already existent in the natural and human worlds. The sage commander is its central figure, a general who combines military acumen with the role of wisdom holder from the old high culture. Thus it embeds military thinking in the sophisticated philosophical debates then sweeping China.

This text is complexly responsive to unique conditions of the Warring States. It therefore demands to be understood in those terms. Can we then read it in other contexts without severely distorting or dismembering it? How do we distinguish its culture-bound content from its farther-reaching implications?

The *Sun Tzu* is unusual in that it offers us several means by which we may successfully overcome these conditions. As we have seen, it teaches a view of the whole, a perspective one might assume on the workings of any world, not just Warring States China. Its contents are historically specific, but they function as illustrations of this view rather than as instruction in particular cultural practices. Furthermore, though the *Sun Tzu* maintains an intense dialogue with its intellectual and military environment, it takes no position on the preeminent philosophical issues of its time. True knowledge, it insists, arises only in the moment: "The victories of the military lineage. . . . cannot be transmitted in advance" (chapter 1).

We can see hints of the *Sun Tzu*'s complex view in its Chinese title, *Ping-fa*. *Ping* means the military, from weapons to soldiers to armies to the strategic principles underlying them all. *Fa* is complex in other ways. It refers to models that can be copied and standards against which things can be measured. From this it comes to mean the proper way to do things. Thus the title might be translated as *Military Methods*, meaning how to act at all levels of the military, employing means that are related to traditional practices but are not mere imitations of them.

In these ways the *Sun Tzu* shifts the focus of knowing from a historically generated text onto our own present circumstances. We need to know its textual history in order to understand how that is possible. But then it demands we leave that story behind. Far from distorting the text, our own questions are the best guide to present action, which is the only place the *Sun Tzu* can come to fruition.

The Emergence of a Text

Some texts are severely structured. They invite us to join their conversation only if we follow a stringent protocol. Writings on math and science are obvious examples of this. If we lose contact after A, B and C, then F, G and R remain mysteries forever. The *Sun Tzu* is quite the opposite. It is a loosely linked set of observations and examples, an assemblage of widely ranging materials with hardly any argumentation at all. And nowhere does it clearly state the set of principles upon which it is based.

Yet certainly the book exhibits striking intelligence and insight. What does its apparent disorganization mean? What must we understand about its structure if we wish to understand its meaning? To answer these questions, it is easiest if we first inquire into how the *Sun Tzu* came to exist as a written work.

According to his biography in the *Records of the Grand Historian*, Sun Tzu was a contemporary of Confucius who served the state of

Wu.[4] There is, however, no historical evidence for this patriarch of East Asian strategy in any records before the third century BCE. It is possible that such a man existed, though we know nothing definite about him. What is certain is that the text that bears his name was not written by the patriarch himself but compiled only years later from oral traditions.

Like nearly all Warring States texts, the *Sun Tzu* is a collection, an anthology created and maintained by members of its lineage. The *Analects* of Confucius is a good example of this practice. It could not have been written by Confucius, since most sections begin "The Master said." Rather it is a record kept by disciples and disciples' disciples. The *Sun Tzu*'s form is similar, most of its thirteen chapters beginning "Master Sun said." How did these collections of oral materials evolve into something that we recognize today as a "book"? What effects did this bookmaking process have on the original material from which it derived? And how does that process affect how we read the *Sun Tzu* today? These are the questions we must next address.[5]

Though we have little direct evidence of Warring States practice, we may imagine an impressive teacher gathering disciples as he propounds a set of doctrine, some inherited or collected from other sources, some original to him. His group maintains itself as a lineage, even after the teacher's death. Their most valued possession is the body of knowledge they preserve and transmit to worthy disciples, perhaps its pith in written form. Subsequent generations may add to this body, as new but consonant materials are generated in response to changing conditions in the world. This newer material is fully melded with the words of the patriarch—and thus in some sense attributable to him. This is possible because his successors have so fully received transmission of his teachings that they can speak from within that tradition. From this perspective the question of forgery does not arise, since there are no significant grounds on which to distinguish the teacher from his successors. It is impossible to locate the modern sense of an "author" anywhere in this process.

At some point an authoritative editor orders this knowledge, perhaps creating the baskets that we will later recognize as "chapters." He may place strong material near the front, adding introductory matters of his own that frame the collection. A written text may then arise, alongside the more fluid oral versions. This process might occur more than once, and the lineage, or its sublineages, may generate new material even after this initial act of editing. By mid–Warring States, more and more written collections of this sort began to appear, and copies of many theretofore private works became available to nonlineage members. Small private libraries became common among the elite. Lineages of disciples increasingly engaged other lineages in debate. The consequences for intellectual development were of course profound.

The form of books in the Warring States period was well suited to such projects. Words were written on strips of bamboo a foot or more long, the strips joined with silk cords and then rolled up. These rolls are called *fascicles*, for "bundle of sticks." It was easy to add text, either at the end of a roll (just tie on more strips of bamboo) or in the form of another fascicle. Sometimes strips were lost when the silk broke. These "books" were expensive to produce and ungainly to store—we have stories of someone's personal collection requiring several oxcarts to transport.

Scholars suspect that the *Sun Tzu* we have today emerged through this process during the second half of the fourth century BCE. Evidence of this assemblage activity is all through the book. Each chapter consists of many short passages. Generally these are connected in theme to the chapter title or topic, but often loosely, and in some sections passages seem totally unrelated. A few sentences appear verbatim in more than one chapter. Stylistically and topically there is strong suggestion of different ages for different parts. The first chapter seems to have been added last, in at least two identifiable stages, as it is addressed to the ruler rather than the general. Perhaps the oldest materials are those found in chapters 8 through 11, which are characterized by typologies and lists of terrain types rather than the conceptually sophisticated materials of earlier chapters. Most important, however, the contents of all chapters are so thoroughly mixed that we can make no such simple discrimination of strata.

The late-fourth-century editing may have produced a text in thirteen fascicles—the number of chapters in the *Sun Tzu* available to us today, called the standard or received text. But the first book cataloging done in China—a survey of the imperial library conducted in the late years BCE—lists the *Sun Tzu* in eighty-two fascicles, sixty-nine more than the standard text. Thus there may have been other parts of the *Sun Tzu* legacy discarded in the most authoritative editing process, or more likely others added material to the collection over the following centuries.

Most of this additional material has been lost. We get hints of it, however, from Chinese encyclopedias of the sixth to twelfth centuries CE, whose military sections frequently quote the *Sun Tzu*. But the texts they quote do not always match the standard text. Some differences are no more than minor variants, but in other instances we find *Sun Tzu* fragments otherwise unknown.[6] Only in the eleventh and twelfth centuries does the tradition narrow, and the works constituting the standard text take their present form. The invention of printing aided in this stabilization.

The Warring States concept of what constituted a proper book thus coincided perfectly with the nature of the *Sun Tzu*. The text is not concerned with argumentation but with establishing a point of view. This view manifests in every passage and from a variety of perspectives. A book culture that demanded linearity would have crippled the *Sun Tzu*. By contrast a composition process that successfully incorporates successive visions allowed it to grow and change without compromising essential structural elements. As a result the power of the text emerges equally from its content and its form.

And then in 1972, against all odds, we were provided special insight into one phase of this process. Archaeologists recovered a text of the *Sun Tzu* from a grave in north China. The tomb was sealed about 130 BCE; its text of the *Sun Tzu* had been written on bamboo strips perhaps fifty years earlier. About 40 percent of the standard text was preserved. There was even a table of contents, written on a wooden board, which named the thirteen chapters. This bamboo text is nearly identical with the *Sun Tzu* that we have today, evidence for the extraordinary fidelity of Chinese textual transmission, its first fifteen hundred years dependent entirely on memorization and the copying of manuscripts.

Despite the general coincidence of bamboo and standard texts, there are some three hundred differences in wording, affecting about 5 percent of the text. Most of these are inconsequential for an English translation, like the distinction between *would* and *might* or a semicolon and a comma. Others affect the quality of language: in the process of transmission, a slightly raw, blunt text was refined, its connections made more explicit, and unpaired items turned into the well-balanced, parallel phrases that classical Chinese prose has esteemed.

In a few instances, however, later editors have actually altered the original meaning of the text. For example, the standard text reads:

> To attack and surely take it, attack where they do
> not defend.
> To defend and surely hold firm, defend where they
> do not attack. [Chapter 6]

The second line parallels the first, and its logic seems clear: if you are defending something that will never be attacked, you will certainly be safe. But the second line of the bamboo text reads:

> To defend and surely hold firm, defend where they
> will surely attack.

On reflection the bamboo text is closer to true military practice. You cannot entirely control where the enemy will attack, but if you know their objective, your preparations can be complete.

In another example the standard text says:

Defend and one is insufficient.
Attack and one has a surplus. [Chapter 4]

This reflects an assumption that one seizes the initiative through attack. But the bamboo text reads:

Defend and one has a surplus.
Attack and one is insufficient.

This acknowledges the danger inherent in any attack and the power of strong preparation in which one awaits the enemy's risky advance. Thus the bamboo text offers a more profound understanding of conflict.

Additionally, the bamboo text demonstrates just how the boundaries of the *Sun Tzu* remained permeable. The standard text received its definitive editing in the fourth century BCE. Thus the list of historical figures in chapter 13 ends about 1000 BCE. But the bamboo text adds the legendary Su Ch'in, who lived perhaps a half century subsequent to that initial fixing of the text. Thus we see that even after its primary compilation, the *Sun Tzu* remained open to further growth, so long as the new material was consonant with its basic principles.

Are these variants the corruptions of a provincial manuscript? No, for in most cases in which the bamboo text differs from the standard, one or more of the medieval encyclopedias attests to the same reading, evidence that the tradition we see in the second century BCE was still alive a thousand years later, lost only in the standardizations of the eleventh and twelfth centuries. Furthermore, the variant readings in the bamboo text are almost always more difficult and shorter, clear indications that they are early—since texts have a well-documented tendency to become more intelligible and longer in the course of their transmission.

For these reasons our translation follows the bamboo text whenever it is available. Its cruder diction is close to the oral tradition from which the *Sun Tzu* had only recently emerged. Its military logic is more profound than that of the standard text and its variant readings unexceptionally strong. Our Web site, www.victoryoverwar.com, reproduces this text in its entirety. It also provides the specific reasoning behind each decision to adopt it in this translation.

If we step back and consider these factors, we realize that what seemed solid—a single object, a book with an author who wrote and published it—turns out to be a series of thoughts over time, linked moments of a process. As a written text, it is held together by the continuity of its transmissions. On a deeper level, it is unified in its perspective, its view of taking whole.

Seeing the text this way has considerable consequences for our relationship with it. Its original process was open and ongoing, something it may be possible to reopen and join, and we can learn to assume its view. Our book is designed so that readers can begin to accomplish such things for themselves. The preceding sections of this essay describe the process, suggesting points at which we may enter it. And we have previously described the view of taking whole. The translation is as close to the Chinese in vocabulary, diction and form as English will allow. In these conditions it is possible to develop an intimate understanding of the text as a living practice. Then, like its earlier lineage holders, we can move outward into the world and act.

Where Are We Now?

Everywhere enormous changes have occurred through the last hundred years. They have grown from within EuroAmerica, they have engulfed and transformed that realm, they have engaged all the rest of the world. These events have brought huge shifts in how we think. As new paradigms have arisen, many elements of the *Sun Tzu* have become recognizable to us—the vision of taking whole, the world understood as relationship. This is one reason that an ancient Chinese text feels so familiar.

These developments have created a basis for the *Sun Tzu* tradition to sustain itself in our contemporary world—not just as a text, which has been known in the West for several centuries, but as practices and a view, as traditions of wisdom. Before turning to military thinking of the last century, we should therefore briefly acknowledge some factors contributing to this culture's ability to comprehend the text. Our objective is to show how thinking in terms of processes has become characteristic of highly diverse sectors of our world. We have chosen only four and do no more than sketch them. Like the *Sun Tzu*, this is a grouping of similar elements rather than an argument. Like our commentary, it seeks to create a ground on which major themes of the text become identifiable.

Natural scientists have altered what we are. Our earth is a dot in space, in motion with its sun through space-time. Our bodies are composed from infinitesimally small pulses of energy. Evolutionary biology shows us our relatedness—at first to mammals but then to single-celled organisms and ultimately to the carbon molecules formed under immense pressures on hydrogen and helium atoms.

The American corporate workplace was once structured by the clockwork of the Newtonian universe. Now we find self-organizing units coordinating with larger groups that operate with a complexity worthy to be called Tao. Knowledge has taken priority over quantifiable resources like land, materials, energy or capital. The market is becoming a conversation that adjusts immediately and spontaneously to every voice, as consumers and producers converge at one spot to design, exchange, utilize and redesign a product in a process that resembles victory.[7]

Asia and EuroAmerica are still discovering each other. The Chinese classics have been translated, bringing the word *Tao* into the English language. With it come religions without a God. Western men and women have undertaken the practices of Buddhism, which sees us as activities without a center, with an inherent buddha nature in place of original sin.

In the process philosophy of Alfred North Whitehead (1861–1947), events, not individuated things, are the fundamental components of reality. Thus we consist only of becomings, and each becoming is a selection made among the countless objects, things and events that went immediately before. Space, time and matter are inseparable. In place of the categories "being, permanence and uniformity," there is only "becoming, change and newness."

Military thinking of the twentieth century parallels these developments in surprising and significant ways. A pair of images from the Great War of 1914–1918 shows how the transformations began. One is of trench armies facing off for years against trench armies in sodden Flanders fields. Stalemate: no one could obtain conclusive shih, and machine guns eliminated those who ventured out. The other image is of T. E. Lawrence, Lawrence of Arabia, slipping across Syria and the Sinai in a very different war against the Turks. His enemy: modern armies with supply trains, headquarters and chains of command. But, he asked,

> suppose we were an influence (as we might be), an idea, a thing invulnerable, intangible, without front or back, drifting about like a gas? Armies were like plants, immobile as a whole, firm-rooted, nourished through long stems to the head. We might be a vapour, blowing where we listed. Our kingdoms lay in each man's mind, and as we wanted nothing material to live on, so perhaps we offered nothing material to the killing.[8]

The trench war disasters opened gaps in long-standing practices of massed frontal assault upon the enemy's center of gravity. Like a deep wound, the gap remained open long enough for Lawrence's friend B. H. Liddell Hart to develop what he would call the indirect approach, an assault that followed the line of least expectation and resistance. And here is synchronicity. In 1927 Liddell Hart received a letter from a British officer serving in China describing the Sun Tzu. The letter drew special attention to the *Sun Tzu*'s image of water, which avoids resistance but in flood will sweep away great boulders. It bore a startling resemblance to Liddell Hart's "expanding torrent" theory, whereby small breaches made in the enemy's defenses would be rapidly followed by a rush of forces expanding behind the enemy's front.

When he published *The British Way in Warfare* five years later, Liddell Hart did not just mix East and West; he used the *Sun Tzu* to transform the ground of European military thinking. The object of war, he argued, is defeat of the adversary, not battle, which is only one means to that end. Success must be sought through deception and by methods that confront the enemy with a dilemma. Victory is not achieved by the physical destruction of the enemy but by their demoralization, which can be accomplished in maneuver. He wrote that the thirteen chapters of the *Sun Tzu* "have never been surpassed in comprehension and depth of understanding. They might well be termed the concentrated essence of wisdom on the conduct of war."[9] Indeed, the very term *indirect* translates the Chinese word for "extraordinary."

Vietnam recalled many of these lessons. An impoverished band of peasant farmers defeated the most advanced military organization on earth. Moving through their realm the way a fish swims in water, they "[set] out later than others and arriv[ed] sooner" (chapter 7). By controlling when and how battles would occur, they forced the Americans to prepare against them at every point.

> When I am few and the enemy is many, I can use
> the few to strike the many because those with
> whom I do battle are restricted!
>
> The ground on which I do battle with him cannot
> be known.
> Then the enemy's preparations are many.
> When his preparations are many, I battle the few!
> [Chapter 6]

General Vo Nguyen Giap had studied the *Sun Tzu*, but "my fighting gospel is T. E. Lawrence's *Seven Pillars of Wisdom*."[10] After 1968 he avoided large-scale confrontation with U.S. forces, choosing instead to mire the Americans in a drawn-out and indecisive lunging after his dispersed troops. As Lawrence had previously written, war on such as Giap "is messy and slow, like eating soup with a knife."[11]

Perhaps there is a causal connection between that experience and the 1997 edition of the United States Marine Corps' *Warfighting* manual. There is certainly a connection between the latter and the *Sun Tzu*, which it quotes extensively. Against the memory of Teddy Roosevelt leading his Rough Riders up San Juan Hill in 1898, we have the *Warfighting* manual arguing one century later that

> an appreciation for surfaces and gaps requires a certain amount of judgment. What is a surface in one case may be a gap in another. For example, a forest which is a surface to an armored unit because it restricts vehicle movement can be a gap to an infantry unit which can infiltrate through it. . . . If our main effort has struck a surface but another unit has located a gap, we designate the second unit as the main effort and redirect our combat power in support of it. In this manner, we "pull" combat power through gaps from the front rather than "pushing" it through from the rear.

Thus, in a seeming combination of Whitehead and the *Sun Tzu*, the *Warfighting* manual states:

> Like friction and uncertainty, fluidity is an inherent attribute of war. Each episode in war is the temporary result of a unique combination of circumstances, presenting a unique set of problems and requiring an original solution. Nevertheless, no episode can be viewed in isolation. Rather, each episode merges with those that precede and

follow it—shaped by the former and shaping the conditions of the latter—creating a continuous, fluctuating
flow of activity replete with fleeting opportunities and
unforeseen events. Since war is a fluid phenomenon, its
conduct requires flexibility of thought. Success depends
in large part on the ability to adapt—to proactively shape
changing events to our advantage as well as to react
quickly to constantly changing conditions.

In sum:

It should be clear that maneuver warfare exists not so
much in the specific methods used—we do not believe
in a formularistic approach to war—but in the mind of
the Marine.[12]

This is an extraordinary event within a series of extraordinary events. The *Sun Tzu* has conquered us in just the way it
recommends—by taking whole, bringing us around to a larger
view. We choose freely to come because its wisdom is now our
wisdom. And in a still more profound conquest, just as General
Giap took T. E. Lawrence as his mentor, the book's unstated
assumptions—change, interrelatedness, taking whole—have
become as apparent today as they were twenty-five hundred years
ago in China. The *Sun Tzu* has successfully infiltrated EuroAmerican culture because so many of its key perspectives had been
adopted here in advance. The environment it depends on to fully
manifest is now present.

When ancient traditions are authentically joined, they
become present traditions. As present tradition the *Sun Tzu* is one
part of contemporary world culture, itself centerless, at any
moment new and endlessly transforming. Rather than being the
property only of an ancient lineage, the *Sun Tzu* is everywhere
in the world, as when

the five spies arise together and no one knows
　　　their Tao,
This is what is meant by "spiritlike web."
　　　[Chapter 13]

The text is alive, and it will change as you, the reader, mix your own wisdom with it. These are the victories of the military lineage. They cannot be transmitted in advance.

PART THREE

Commentary

ANCIENT CHINESE TEXTS ARE OFTEN DIFFICULT TO UNDERSTAND, even for an educated Chinese reader. All classics were therefore accompanied by commentaries, which were relied on to elucidate difficult passages or establish authoritative interpretation. In keeping with that tradition, this commentary provides information we feel may be helpful in working with the *Sun Tzu*. Like our predecessors, we supply background materials from Chinese language and history. We also identify important terms on their first appearance. However, we stop short of providing final meanings. Instead we trust that as each key word or theme recurs, its meaning will clarify and deepen, as when discovering new facets of an intricately cut gem. In the same spirit, while we bring out patterns of thought essential to the text, we leave open how this wisdom might apply in any individual situation. Throughout we assume that the perspective of victory through taking whole underlies all passages of the text.

I

Appraisals

SUN TZU SAID:

The military is a great matter of the state.
It is the ground of death and life,
The Tao of survival or extinction.
One cannot but examine it.

The military provides protection. Although the *Sun Tzu* arose in relation to the political state, its logic applies to every form of life, for the function of protection is crucial to them all. Protection means respecting one's integrity, through either warding off or extending outward—through defending or conquering. It may entail conflict. Regardless of whether we find these functions pleasant, we must look into them.

And so base it in the five.
Compare by means of the appraisals.
Thus seek out its nature.

Addressed to the ruler, this chapter discusses the five factors and seven appraisals by which one can assess the military.

> The first is Tao, the second is heaven, the third is
> earth, the fourth is the general, the fifth is
> method.

"The five" are the well-known triad of heaven, earth and humanity, flanked by Tao and method. Thus the *Sun Tzu* announces its engagement with the major elements of Warring States thought and at the same time its application beyond the field of military action. These five are a whole, inseparable in forming the basis of the military.

> Tao is what causes the people to have the same
> purpose as their superior.
> Thus they can die with him, live with him and
> not deceive him.

Tao is a roadway, a path, the way something works and equally a recommended course of action, the way something should be done. As a verb it means "to lead," and thus "leadership." All these meanings are present here.

The word translated "causes" is also the common term for a military order. Here it indicates the way in which leader and led become of a single mind. This unity cannot be imposed from without. It arises when all are in tune with the larger order, the Tao, the way things work.

"And not deceive him." The standard texts conclude this line with some variant of "and not be anxious." The bamboo text is much stronger, since this passage concerns the unity of purpose, even to death, among one's troops. It matters less if they are afraid than if they conceal their state of mind.

> Heaven is yin and yang, cold and hot, the order
> of the seasons.

Going with it, going against it—this is military
victory.

The second line appears only in the bamboo text.

Heaven is not merely the sky or weather. It also represents larger patterns in the universe. "Going with it, going against it" refers to compliance with these processes, which leads to victory. This need not be interpreted as external influence but rather as the general's ability to align his actions with the larger patterns, thereby commanding coincidence.

Earth is high and low, broad and narrow, far and
near, steep and level, death and life.

Just as heaven manifests in many forms, the earth takes varied shapes. These terrains have crucial implications for the military, offering death or life. But earth need not be considered only as physical forms of terrain. It is also the ground of any situation, its practical limitations and opportunities.

The general is knowledge, trustworthiness,
courage and strictness.

The standard text includes the definitive Confucian virtue *jen*, or humaneness, in this list. That term was apparently added by a later editor who hoped to portray the *Sun Tzu* general as a member of Confucian civil society.

The general is the principle of leadership, that which brings together all "the five." His first quality is his knowledge. He is the central figure of the *Sun Tzu*. He is also anyone who would seek to understand this wisdom.

Method is ordering divisions, the Tao of ranking
and principal supply.

"Method" originally referred to something that could be copied, like
a small clay model used in the building of a house. From this it came
to mean standard forms of measurement, such as a quart dipper, which
will always hold the same volume. More generally it indicated any set
of standards and, eventually, the way things could be properly done.
The Chinese title of the text is *Sun Tzu's Military Methods*.

Here methods are the means by which the general structures large
entities and repeatable functions within the military. They give coherence, predictability and strength.

As for all these five—
    No general has not heard of them.
    Knowing them, one is victorious.
    Not knowing them, one is not victorious.

This is the first occurrence in the text of the crucial link between
knowledge and victory.

It is not enough to have heard of these five. One must know them
from the inside. They are the basis of every situation. Fully understood
and integrated, they lead to victory.

And so compare by means of the appraisals.
Thus seek out its nature.

The appraisals are seven ways to determine the state of the military.
Perhaps the *Sun Tzu* once began with this section, since these two lines
appear twice, once here and once near the start of the chapter.

Ask—
> Which ruler has Tao?
> Which general has ability?
> Which attains heaven and earth?
> Which implements method and orders?
> Whose military and multitudes are strong?
> Whose officers and soldiers are trained?
> Whose rewards and punishments are clear?
By these I know victory and defeat!

Whereas "the five" address the foundations of all action, the appraisals are focused more exclusively on military matters. They offer seven bases of comparison between oneself and other. Tao is most important, followed by the general. Absolute standards are unnecessary: the general seeks knowledge by contrasting various qualities, since strength and weakness, self and other, are relative. Thus he knows victory.

> The general heeds my appraisals. Employ him and
> he is certainly victorious. Retain him.
> The general does not heed my appraisals. Employ
> him and he is certainly defeated. Remove him.

Here the *Sun Tzu* addresses the ruler.

The sovereign and his general must be synchronized. The sovereign manifests the vision. The general appraises conditions, determining how that vision can be carried out. Joined together, this makes victory.

> Having appraised the advantages, heed them.
> Then make them into shih to aid with the external.
> Shih is governing the balance according to the
> advantages.

The opening sections of this chapter have shown two ways of assessing the military—using the five and the appraisals. Now it is time to apply that knowledge to external matters. The key means is "shih," the power inherent in a situation.

Through comparisons, we learn where relative advantage lies. We can thus act to bring about a favorable disposition or shih. The shih of any particular situation is constantly changing as conditions shift. It is as if we were placing weights along a beam whose balance point is always in motion. From knowledge gained through the appraisals, the fulcrum is more readily found.

————————

The military is a Tao of deception—
    Thus when able, manifest inability.
    When active, manifest inactivity.
    When near, manifest as far.
    When far, manifest as near.
    Thus when he seeks advantage, lure him. ⁓
    When he is in chaos, take him. ⁓
    When he is substantial, prepare against him. ⁓
    When he is strong, avoid him. ⁓
    When he is wrathful, harass him.
    Attack where he is unprepared.
    Emerge where he does not expect it.

Four of these lines are in four-word, rhymed couplets, the diction of China's oldest poetry and a common feature of Warring States texts.

The following three lines appear in the standard but not the bamboo text:

    When he is humble, make him proud. ⁓
    When he is at ease, make him labor. ⁓
    When he is in kinship, separate him. ⁓

Deception is a means to become formless, invisible, unimaginable, or to appear as somewhere or something one is not. If we are not discernible to the enemy, they cannot prepare against us. If they cannot tell where we are, we could arise anywhere.

Knowing the enemy's tendencies and momentum, it becomes simple to lure them, take them or prepare against them. If they are occupied with responding to our initiatives, they become unable to mount their own.

These are the victories of the military lineage.
They cannot be transmitted in advance.

Victories depend on shih, whose configuration is never constant. The general must recognize a momentary advantage, capturing victory as it arises. These victories cannot be set aside for future use, nor can they be taught.

Now, in the rod-counting at court before battle,
    one is victorious who gets many counting
    rods.
In the rod-counting at court before battle, one is
    not victorious who gets few counting rods.
Many counting rods is victorious over few counting
    rods,
How much more so over no counting rods.
By these means I observe them.
Victory and defeat are apparent.

We know little about this calculation. Some historians presume it was done on the basis of the seven appraisals, with strong positions receiving rods or tallies, but this is only speculation. Other contemporaneous texts speak of rod-counting in the royal court or temple. In those instances it may have been a form of divination, though the *Sun Tzu* is explicit that foreknowledge cannot be obtained in this way.

From knowledge gained through the appraisals, one can know victory. But the particular means by which victory will be attained depend on the general's skill in battle. Though victory may be known in advance, the ever-changing shih of battle exist only in the moment.

2

Doing Battle

SUN TZU SAID:

In sum, the method of employing the military—

With one thousand fast chariots, one thousand
leather-covered chariots and one hundred
thousand armored troops to be provisioned
over one thousand li—
then expenses of outer and inner, stipends of
foreign advisers, materials for glue and
lacquer, and contributions for chariots and
armor are one thousand gold pieces a day.
Only after this are one hundred thousand soldiers
raised.

Mounting an army requires enormous resources. These expenses
are unavoidable if you seek to do battle. Calculations here are not simply financial. The general is concerned with economy in its largest
sense. This includes the complex balance of forces in which every
aspect of the state, including social and moral life, is affected.

———————

When one employs battle—
 If victory takes long, it blunts the military and
  grinds down its sharpness.
 Attacking walled cities, one's strength is
  diminished.
 If soldiers are long in the field, the state's
  resources are insufficient.

Now if one blunts the military, grinds down its
  sharpness,
Diminishes its strength and exhausts its goods,
Then the feudal lords ride one's distress and rise up.
Even one who is wise cannot make good the
  aftermath!

Thus in the military one has heard of foolish speed
  but has not observed skillful prolonging.
And there has never been a military prolonging
  that has brought advantage to the state.

The feudal lords were rulers of the many states of north China. In the *Sun Tzu*, they are portrayed as unreliable allies who will swiftly transform into opportunistic enemies.

The initial expense of bringing an army to battle is huge, and prolongation only magnifies it. Then your diminished resources create a new vulnerability. Nothing can protect you from this. If victory cannot be quickly attained, it is destructive to attempt it.

The conventional use of force demands concerted effort. That grinds down the enemy, but it also blunts your own sharpness. This is prolongation, in which one mistakes the intensity of engagement for the path to victory. Although speed in battle can be misapplied, it is difficult for prolongation to bring advantage.

And so one who does not thoroughly know the
  harm from employing the military ∼

Cannot thoroughly know the advantage from
employing the military. ～

The use of military force is always destructive, to oneself as well as to the other. The general who ignores this will not know how to use the army to advantage, nor the particular advantages in using an army at all. He must be aware of every way that things can go wrong.

The skillful general recognizes how harm can bring advantage, how the enemy's advantage may not bring him harm, how easily these can invert. By seeing the interdependence of advantage and harm, self and other, he moves to victory.

———————

One skilled at employing the military
Does not have a second registering of conscripts nor
    a third loading of grain.
One takes equipment from the state and relies on
    grain from the enemy.
Thus the army's food can be made sufficient.

When doing battle, avoid the extra burden of creating, transporting, maintaining and consuming your own wealth. Instead, take advantage of goods that are already at hand. Thus the enemy's resources are used to defeat them.

———————

A state's impoverishment from its soldiers—
    When they are distant, there is distant transport.
    When they are distant and there is distant
        transport, the hundred clans are impoverished.
    When soldiers are near, things sell dearly.
    When things sell dearly, wealth is exhausted.
    When wealth is exhausted, people are hard-
        pressed by local taxes.

Diminished strength in the heartland,
Emptiness in the households.
Of the hundred clans' resources, six-tenths is
    gone.
Of the ruling family's resources—
    Broken chariots, worn-out horses, ～
    Armor, helmets, arrows, crossbows, ～
    Halberds, shields, spears, pavises, ～
    Heavy ox-drawn wagons— ～
Seven-tenths is gone.

Thus the wise general looks to the enemy for food.
One bushel of enemy food equals twenty bushels of
    mine.
One bale of fodder equals twenty bales of mine.

The impoverishment of battle reaches to every part of the economy.
It not only affects material goods but also frays the social fabric. The
general does not burden the state because he obtains his food and supplies from the enemy.

And so killing the enemy is a matter of wrath.
Taking the enemy's goods is a matter of advantage.

Finding the right motivation, it is easy to get your troops either to kill
or to take. But the economy of battle values the good use of both lives
and material resources. Living off the enemy brings one closer to victory.

And so in chariot battles—
    When more than ten chariots are captured,
    Reward him who first captures one.
    Then change their flags and pennants.

When the chariots are mixed together, ride them.
Supply the captives and care for them.
This is what is meant by "victorious over the enemy
and so increasing one's strength."

Enemy equipment can be captured and turned against them. Give a chariot to the first person to take one in battle, fit it with your insignia and integrate it into your forces.

But food and equipment are not the only resources the general obtains from the enemy. He must win over their people as well. His strength increases when he brings the enemy around to the larger perspective.

And so the military values victory.
It does not value prolonging.

This passage is an initial summary of the chapter.

Victory means taking whole. Battle is costly. When prolonged, it is devastating to all. If battle is necessary, it must be quick.

And so the general who knows the military is the
people's fate star,
The ruler of the state's security and danger.

The fate star controls the time of death. This is a final summation of the chapter.

Knowledge of the military shows the general how to use the enemy's resources, avoid prolongation and find victory. That knowledge also gives him power to preserve or destroy the state. This is the largest economy, which extends far past battle. It ranges from natural principles in the heavens to the cost of glue, lacquer and grain.

3

Strategy of Attack

SUN TZU SAID:

In sum, the method of employing the military—

Taking a state whole is superior.
Destroying it is inferior to this.

Taking an army whole is superior.
Destroying it is inferior to this.

Taking a battalion whole is superior.
Destroying it is inferior to this.

Taking a company whole is superior.
Destroying it is inferior to this.

Taking a squad whole is superior.
Destroying it is inferior to this.

Therefore, one hundred victories in one hundred
battles is not the most skillful.

Subduing the other's military without battle is the
most skillful.

The skillful general conquers the enemy without destroying them.
"Taking whole" leaves them intact, transforms them. It builds upon
itself. By contrast "one hundred victories" places battle at the center,
ignoring the fact that conflict may lead to further conflict. This principle extends from the greatest to the smallest.

This is not an argument against the use of force. Instead it sees battle in the context of victory.

And so the superior military cuts down strategy.
Its inferior cuts down alliances.
Its inferior cuts down the military.
The worst attacks walled cities.

The approach of taking whole first targets enemy strategy, undoing
the coherence of their plan. This battle is won in the mind. Next best
is to cut down the enemy's alliances, the connections that hold their
world together. Next, it may be skillful to engage the enemy's forces,
in conventional military fashion. Brute assault is the least effective.

This military is the protector of the state's integrity, seeking victory
rather than conquest.

The method of attacking walled cities—
    Ready the siege towers and armored vehicles.
    This is completed after three months.
    Pile up the earthworks.
    This also takes three months.
    If the general is not victorious over his anger
        and sets them swarming like ants,

> One-third of the officers and soldiers are killed
> and the walled city not uprooted—
> This is the calamity of attack.

Strategy manuals sometimes provide detailed instruction on the methods of siege. Here instead we see the wastefulness of blunt aggression, which consumes time, money, property and lives. Furthermore, attacking the civilian homes of the enemy creates conditions that diminish any chance of taking whole.

Aggression not only devastates enemy resources. It may also overcome the general, cloud his judgment and draw him further into destruction and loss.

> And so one skilled at employing the military
>> Subdues the other's military but does not do
>> battle,
>> Uproots the other's walled city but does not
>> attack,
>> Destroys the other's state but does not prolong.
> One must take it whole when contending for all-
> under-heaven.
> Thus the military is not blunted and advantage can
> be whole.
> This is the method of the strategy of attack.

The first four lines summarize the chapter so far.

Only with the strategy of taking whole will the general find complete victory. This means assuming the perspective of the whole at the outset of the campaign. Thus you keep your military intact, preserving both the advantage that leads to victory and the advantage that comes from victory.

At times you may have to destroy the enemy's state. If so, do it quickly. There is no simple rule on this.

And so the method of employing the military—
    When ten to one, surround them.
    When five to one, attack them.
    When two to one, do battle with them.
    When matched, then divide them.
    When fewer, then defend against them.
    When inadequate, then avoid them.
Thus a small enemy's tenacity ∾
Is a large enemy's catch. ∾

The standard text says, "When two to one, then divide them. When matched, then be able to battle them." This is inconsistent with the *Sun Tzu*'s logic, and following certain early texts, we have inverted these two phrases.[1]

Though it is better to take whole and avoid conflict, sometimes battle is necessary. In each case the best strategy will arise from your particular circumstances. Assess the enemy's strength relative to your own and respond accordingly.

Attachment to any strategy, however good, leads to defeat. The general may flee from battle if the larger victory demands it.

Now the general is the safeguard of the state.
If the safeguard is complete, the state is surely strong.
If the safeguard is flawed, the state is surely weak.

Here "the state" is the final good, the entity whose integrity must be maintained. The general is its protector. Only when he is fully accomplished does he ensure its welfare.

And so the sovereign brings adversity to the army
in three ways—

Not knowing the army is unable to advance yet
ordering an advance,
Not knowing the army is unable to retreat yet
ordering a retreat,
This is what is meant by "hobbling the army."

Not knowing affairs within the three armies yet
controlling the governance of the three armies,
Then the army's officers are confused!

Not knowing the three armies' balance yet
controlling appointments in the three armies,
Then the army's officers are distrustful!

Once the three armies are confused and distrustful,
Troubles from the feudal lords intensify!
This is what is meant by "an army in chaos leads to
victory."

The "three armies" refer to divisions of center, left and right within
the larger body of troops. They indicate all the forces of the state.

The sovereign calls upon the general to act. But skillful action
depends on the authority that comes from knowledge. Knowledge arises
from the situation at hand. Lacking this knowledge, a sovereign who
interferes in military activities creates chaos. An army in chaos leads
to victory for the enemy.

———————

And so knowing victory is fivefold—
Knowing when one can and cannot do battle is
victory.
Knowing the use of the many and the few is
victory.

Superior and inferior desiring the same is victory.
Being prepared and awaiting the unprepared is
victory.
The general being capable and the ruler not
interfering is victory.
These five are a Tao of knowing victory.

Knowing victory means being able to nurture those conditions that determine victory. It depends on the mastery of many disciplines: the moment of pulling the trigger, the use of varied troop strength, morale, waiting and the proper relations between general and ruler. These five must become a single, inexhaustible way to victory.

And so in the military—
Knowing the other and knowing oneself, ∼
In one hundred battles no danger. ∼
Not knowing the other and knowing oneself, ∼
One victory for one loss. ∼
Not knowing the other and not knowing
oneself, ∼
In every battle certain defeat. ∼

Knowledge protects one from danger. The general must know both self and other, conditions here and conditions there. This requires an ability to penetrate all aspects of the world.

Victory comes from taking whole. It includes both self and other in a single vision.

4

Form

SUN TZU SAID:

Of old the skilled first made themselves invincible
   to await the enemy's vincibility.

Invincibility lies in oneself.
Vincibility lies in the enemy.

Thus the skilled can make themselves invincible.
They cannot cause the enemy's vincibility.

Thus it is said, "Victory can be known. It cannot be
   made."

Elsewhere the *Sun Tzu* gives explicit advice about "making victory."
Here, though, it emphasizes one's ground of action—preparing the conditions of invincibility within one's own sphere. This is not yet victory. One must wait for the enemy's vincibility to arise. Skill is knowing
that moment.

Invincibility is defense.
Vincibility is attack.

Defend and one has a surplus.
Attack and one is insufficient.

The standard text says, "Attack when you have a surplus; defend when you are insufficient." This logic maintains the convention of gaining victory through attack. The bamboo text points to the vulnerability of attack and the subtle power of defense.

Of old those skilled at defense hid below the nine
    earths and moved above the nine heavens.
Thus they could preserve themselves and be
    all-victorious.

Here the standard text has: "One skilled at defense hides below the nine earths; one skilled at attack moves above the nine heavens." This obscures the more powerful message of the bamboo text, which shows instead a defense not based in conflict.

In the best defense, one goes outside the range of enemy insight, becoming ungraspable and thus unbeatable. Victory need not be achieved by will or devastation. The all-victorious general resides beyond defeat.

In seeing victory, not going beyond what everyone
    knows is not skilled.
Victory in battle that all-under-heaven calls skilled
    is not skilled.
Thus lifting an autumn hair does not mean great
    strength.
Seeing the sun and the moon does not mean a clear eye.
Hearing thunder does not mean a keen ear.
So-called skill is to be victorious over the easily
    defeated.

Thus the battles of the skilled are without
extraordinary victory, without reputation for
wisdom and without merit for courage.

According to Chinese lore, the downy coats of birds and animals are especially fine at the onset of fall.

The standard text says, "What is meant by skill is to be victorious over the easily defeated." It implies that the skilled general fights only those he can readily beat—and thus develops no reputation for greatness.

The bamboo text comes to the same conclusion, but for different reasons. What most people can see is not skill. True skill is both invisible to ordinary people and achieves more than they can envision. Thus the general's victories are unknown.

———————

And so one's victories are without error.
Being without error, what one arranges is
necessarily victorious
Since one is victorious over the defeated.

One skilled at battle takes a stand in the ground of
no defeat
And so does not lose the enemy's defeat.
Therefore, the victorious military is first victorious
and after that does battle.
The defeated military first does battle and after that
seeks victory.

For the skilled general, victory is attained before the battle is joined. Abiding in his invincibility, he awaits the moment at which he can seize the enemy's vincibility. A military that rushes to the fight, hoping for victory, assumes the ground of defeat.

———————

And so one who is skilled cultivates Tao and
    preserves method.
Thus one can be the measure of victory and defeat.

Tao is the way things are, the way things go of their own accord,
the natural momentum. Method is ordering human actions in ways that
are in accord with Tao. The general assumes this power when he is
tuned in to the larger perspective, thus becoming the governor of victory and defeat.

As for method—
    First, measure length.
    Second, measure volume.
    Third, count.
    Fourth, weigh.
    The fifth is victory.

    Earth gives birth to length.
    Length gives birth to volume.
    Volume gives birth to counting.
    Counting gives birth to weighing.
    Weighing gives birth to victory.

Method gives rise to victory because it is in direct contact with the
phenomenal world. Here that is done through calculations. First, measure the linear, the two-dimensional. Second, measure volume, the
three-dimensional. Third, determine how many fill that space. Fourth,
weigh the potentials. The fifth is victory. Because the world is fully
interconnected, each calculation is linked necessarily to its successor.
    Conflict is made up of small details. If one can see the depth and
subtlety of measurable things, then victory is not mysterious.

A victorious military is like weighing a
      hundredweight against a grain.
A defeated military is like weighing a grain against
      a hundredweight.
One who weighs victory sets the people to battle
      like releasing amassed water into a gorge one
      thousand jen deep.

This is form.

Because you have taken the measure of things, you know their true weight. Victory is then arranging the balance to create preponderance. Like the release of water down a steep ravine, this is shih.

5

Shih

Ordering the many is like ordering the few.
It is division and counting.

Fighting the many is like fighting the few.
It is form and name.

The Chinese character for "ordering" suggests regulating or properly arranging. When you give order to the many, when the large is divided into the small, working with the many becomes like working with the few. When you form troops into clearly named divisions, fighting with the many is no different from fighting with the few. The same principles apply, activated by the same gestures. As well, interacting with the small, you establish connections that accumulate power as you build to the large. Thus you command the vastness by working with the manageable and immediate—that which is right in front of you. This is effective on all levels of command.

The multitude of the three armies can be made to
meet all enemies without defeat.
It is the extraordinary and the orthodox.

"The orthodox" translates the Chinese word *cheng*. Its original meaning, at least a thousand years before the *Sun Tzu*, was "straight," and thus "correct." From these senses evolved the term *to govern*. "The orthodox," then, is the right way to do things according to public measures. In social life it would indicate conventional good form. "The extraordinary" is literally "the strange." It has none of the political associations of the orthodox.

In general, the orthodox is the familiarity of our world, the ways in which we engage reality, the way our senses normally work. It is what we and the enemy expect. For the military, it is accepted means and models. It may also include conventional strategy and tactics.

The extraordinary is always surprising. It is not defined as any particular action. It is simply what the enemy does not expect.

How a military comes to prevail, like throwing a
        grindstone against an egg.
It is the empty and the solid.

The military conquers through preponderance. Concentrate your force at the empty point, where your enemy cannot resist.

In sum, when in battle,
Use the orthodox to engage.
Use the extraordinary to attain victory.

Engage people with what they expect. It is what they are able to discern and confirms their projections. It settles them into predictable patterns of response, occupying their minds while you wait for the extraordinary moment—that which they cannot anticipate.

The orthodox prepares the ground for the possibility of the extraordinary. Only through complete training in the conventions of your craft are you able to recognize subtle variations in your enemy's practice of it and respond immediately to them.

The extraordinary is unanticipated, but the orthodox is not fixed either. It changes as people's perceptions grow and shift. Use of these two thus requires constant awareness of the enemy's developing state of mind. It is a contemplative exercise, not a repeatable trick.

———————

And so one skilled at giving rise to the
    extraordinary—

As boundless as heaven and earth,
As inexhaustible as the Yellow River and the
    ocean.

Ending and beginning again,
It is the sun and the moon.

Dying and then being born,
It is the four seasons.

The general gives rise to the extraordinary—literally, "gives birth" to it. He does not create or assemble it. Uncreated, it is inexhaustible, like heaven and earth. Like cycles of the natural world, large beyond human reach, it ends but begins again.

———————

Musical pitches do not exceed five,
Yet all their variations cannot be heard.

Colors do not exceed five,
Yet all their variations cannot be seen.

Tastes do not exceed five,
Yet all their variations cannot be tasted.

The shih of battle do not exceed the extraordinary
    and the orthodox,
Yet all their variations cannot be exhausted.

The extraordinary and the orthodox circle and give
        birth to each other,
As a circle has no beginning.
Who is able to exhaust it?

Five pitches combine to make all music. Every amazing sight in our world derives from only five colors. Out of finite elements, an endless display emerges. In the same way, the many shih of battle are a matter only of the extraordinary and orthodox.

Knowing this, one can discern the simple patterns that lie within the overwhelming multiplicity of phenomena. Mastering the extraordinary and orthodox, one can create shih inexhaustibly.

The extraordinary and orthodox give birth to each other. They are interdependent. What is extraordinary now may soon become orthodox. An apparently orthodox action may be what your adept opponent least expects from you. Thus the extraordinary and orthodox depend entirely on our conception of them.

The rush of water, to the point of tossing rocks
        about. This is shih.
The strike of a hawk, at the killing snap. This is
        the node.

Therefore, one skilled at battle—
        His shih is steep.
        His node is short.

Shih is like drawing the crossbow.
The node is like pulling the trigger.

Shih is the power inherent in a configuration. It does not rely solely on powerful components. As Lao Tzu says, water is the softest thing in the world, yet here it tosses rocks about. This water is powerful because it has come together in a particular conformation, cascading through the ravine.

The node is that small juncture between the sections of bamboo. It indicates the abrupt moment at which something occurs—the present, between past and future. It must be short: its target is always in motion.

The power of shih comes from combining these two elements. When you pull the trigger of a crossbow, its gradually accumulated energy is released all at once, in one spot.

Pwun-pwun. Hwun-hwun.
The fight is chaotic yet one is not subject to chaos.

Hwun-hwun. Dwun-dwun.
One's form is round and one cannot be defeated.

Pwun-hwun indicates tangled cords and the confusion of battle. *Hwun-dwun* is the word for a whole whose pieces cannot be individually identified. Roundness suggests completeness.

In chaotic conditions the usual patterns, which constitute the orthodox world, are not discernible. One order has gone, and the next has not yet arisen. Chaos thus offers continual openings to someone who can perceive a deeper order.

One's form is round because all possibilities are included in it. One can respond without confusion to whatever emerges. Thus one cannot be defeated.

Chaos is born from order.
Cowardice is born from bravery.
Weakness is born from strength.

Order and chaos are a matter of counting.
Bravery and cowardice are a matter of shih.
Strength and weakness are a matter of form.

"Counting" stands for "division and counting." It refers to dividing one's army into smaller, manageable groups. Placing your army in proper conditions of shih brings out its natural bravery. "Form" indicates troop formations and, more generally, any shaping of forces.

Cowardice and bravery are two moments of a single cycle. Instead of manipulating one part of the cycle, shape the environment using counting, shih or form, and the quality you seek readily occurs.

———————

One skilled at moving the enemy
    Forms and the enemy must follow,
    Offers and the enemy must take.
Move them by this and await them with troops.

Do not fight the enemy head-on. Instead, shape their ground. This narrows the enemy's course of action, leading them where you want. They have no alternative. If your offer is made from the perspective of victory, they choose it as if it were their own idea. This is skill.

———————

And so one skilled at battle
Seeks it in shih and does not demand it of people.
Thus one can dispense with people and employ
    shih.

Victory does not come from accumulating troop strength or creating heroism. Rather, bring about advantageous shih to shape the field of battle. In the defile one person stands off one hundred. In winter the enemy's impassable river becomes your road of ice.

Relying on shih, the battle of army against army need not occur. This is the highest skill. It is victory.

———————

One who uses shih sets people to battle as if rolling
     trees and rocks.
As for the nature of trees and rocks—
    When still, they are at rest.
    When agitated, they move.
    When square, they stop.
    When round, they go.
Thus the shih of one skilled at setting people to
     battle is like rolling round rocks from a
     mountain one thousand jen high.

This is shih.

The mountain, like the crossbow, emphasizes the potential-energy aspect of shih.

Victory is not based solely on the quality of your people or their strength of will. Thus there is no need to remake or alter them. If you know their nature, you can position them so that they become natural weapons. Thus you take advantage of the way power arises in the world.

6

The Solid and Empty

One who takes position first at the battleground
    and awaits the enemy is at ease.
One who takes position later at the battleground
    and hastens to do battle is at labor.
Thus one skilled at battle summons others and is
    not summoned by them.

How one can make the enemy arrive of their own
    accord—offer them advantage.
How one can prevent the enemy from arriving—
    harm them.
Thus how one can make the enemy labor when at
    ease and starve when full—emerge where
    they must hasten.

Arrive first at the place of battle, gain the initiative and wait. You have shaped the conflict, bringing the enemy to the battlefield of your choice. Offer real or imagined advantage to move them, threaten real or imagined harm to restrict them.

Because you appear unexpectedly at a vital point, the enemy must rush to meet you. Hurried, they labor. Laboring, they are insufficient. These are mental as much as physical conditions. They divert the enemy's attention and cloud their vision.

To go one thousand li without fear, go through
   unpeopled ground.
To attack and surely take it, attack where they do
   not defend.
To defend and surely hold firm, defend where they
   will surely attack.

Thus with one skilled at attack, the enemy does not
   know where to defend.
With one skilled at defense, the enemy does not
   know where to attack.

The standard text reads, "To defend and surely hold firm, defend where they will not attack." At first glance this looks wise: you are promised a secure defense because the enemy does not attack you there. But a perfectly defended fortress that no one wishes to attack is simply irrelevant. Furthermore, the bamboo text has a stronger logic: you cannot entirely control where the enemy will attack, but if you know in advance the location of their attack, your defense can be secure.

When advancing, move through open space—any ground that is unnoticed or uncontested. In attack find the enemy's unguarded moment. In defense, knowing their objective, hold strong at the point of their attack. They will know neither where to defend nor where to attack.

Subtle! Subtle!
To the point of formlessness. ∾
Spiritlike! Spiritlike!
To the point of soundlessness. ∾
Thus one can be the enemy's fate star. ∾

An ancient Chinese ode says, "Heaven is soundless, odorless." The fate star controls the time of death.

If you are formless and soundless, your movement and intentions are invisible to the enemy. If you synchronize your actions with natural processes, your power is predominant.

> To advance so that one cannot be resisted, charge
>> against the empty.
> To retreat so that one cannot be stopped, go so far
>> that one cannot be reached.
>
> And so if I wish to do battle, the enemy cannot but
>> do battle with me.
> I attack what he must save.
>
> If I do not wish to do battle, I mark a line on the
>> earth to defend it, and the enemy cannot do
>> battle with me.
> I misdirect him.

You reach your objective with ease if you encounter no resistance. Find the open way, that which the enemy does not defend or even notice. Your advance or attack is successful because it is directed at an unguarded target.

In retreat remove yourself beyond reach. In battle attack the enemy's vital point. If you wish to avoid battle, cause your enemy to believe that you are invulnerable. Your confidence is so imposing that they cannot trust their own perceptions.

> And so the skilled general forms others yet is
>> without form.
> Hence I am concentrated and the enemy is divided.
> I am concentrated and thus one.
> The enemy is divided and thus one-tenth.
> This is using one-tenth to strike one.

You dictate the enemy's form and manifestation while remaining formless yourself. Thus you keep your focus and remain strong, while they must split their strength against you.

When I am few and the enemy is many, I can use
the few to strike the many because those with
whom I do battle are restricted!

The ground on which I do battle with him cannot
be known.
Then the enemy's preparations are many.
When his preparations are many, I battle the few!

Prepare the front and the rear has few.
Prepare the left and the right has few.
Everywhere prepared, everywhere few.

The few are those who prepare against others.
The many are those who make others prepare
against them.

The standard texts all say, "When I am many and the enemy is few, I can use the many to strike the few." The bamboo text inverts this.

Though outnumbered, you still can attack. The enemy is formed by you: they must prepare against you on all sides. Thus even your smaller force outnumbers that portion of their troops you engage. In this way you make their many few.

You are prepared for everything because your preparation is not focused on any single possibility.

Knowing the battle day and knowing the
battleground,

One can go one thousand li and do battle.
Not knowing the battle day and not knowing the
　　battleground,
The front cannot help the rear, the rear cannot
　　help the front,
The left cannot help the right, the right cannot
　　help the left.
How much more so when the far is several tens of li
　　and the near is several li away!

You attain victory even when starting from far away because you know the objective, the time and place of battle. This does not depend only on advance knowledge. It is also determined by making others prepare against you. Lacking this knowledge, your command is in disarray.

———————

Though by my estimate the military of Yueh is many,
How does this further victory?

Thus it is said, "Victory can be usurped."
Although the enemy is numerous, they can be kept
　　from fighting.

Yueh was the populous state of southeastern China, the mortal enemy of Wu, where Sun Tzu is said to have served.

"Victory can be usurped." The Chinese word for *usurped* has the sense of "turned" but also of taking something that is not properly one's own. The standard text reads, "Victory can be made." A later editor apparently felt the need to soften the text.

Though many troops may be an asset, they do not by themselves assure success. Fewer troops with greater strategy can take a victory not apparently theirs.

———————

And so prick them and know the pattern of their
    movement and stillness.
Form them and know the ground of death and life.
Appraise them and know the plans for gain and
    loss.
Probe them and know the places of surplus and
    insufficiency.

True knowledge of the enemy comes from active contact, which the
general initiates and conducts. He provokes them to reveal themselves,
assessing the full extent of their reactions and resources.

———————

The ultimate in giving form to the military is to
    arrive at formlessness.
When one is formless, deep spies cannot catch a
    glimpse and the wise cannot strategize.

Your form cannot be assessed by spies or strategists because there is
nothing there for them to grasp. Thus they are formed by their own projections, which is all they can discern. These projections, in turn, reveal
their position to you. This is a Tao of deception.

———————

Rely on form to bring about victory over the
    multitude,
And the multitude cannot understand.
The elite all know the form by which I am
    victorious,
But no one knows how I determine the form of
    victory.
Do not repeat the means of victory,
But respond to form from the inexhaustible.

Ordinary people see the victory but not the form by which it is achieved. The elite understand the form of victory but not how that form arose. The general, free from fixation on particular means, responds inexhaustibly to each new situation.

Now the form of the military is like water.
Water in its movement avoids the high and hastens
      to the low.
The military in its victory avoids the solid and
      strikes the empty.
Thus water determines its movement in accordance
      with the earth.
The military determines victory in accordance with
      the enemy.
The military is without fixed shih and without
      lasting form.

To be able to transform with the enemy is what is
      meant by "spiritlike."

This is the initial summary of the chapter.

The essential quality of the all-victorious military is that it has no fixed form. This is its power, that it manifests in whatever way is required to attain victory, spiritlike, transforming without obstacle, without hesitation. It takes shape in response to what is given—the enemy, their disposition, the terrain, any aspect of battle.

Of the Five Phases, none is the lasting victor.
Of the four seasons, none has constant rank.
The sun shines short and long.
The moon dies and lives.

In the conquest cycle of the Five Phases, water overcomes fire, which in turn overcomes wood, which overcomes metal, which overcomes earth, which overcomes water.

The phenomenal world is in constant transformation, yet there are patterns within it. Holding to any single point loses the power of the larger pattern.

Spiritlike essentials.

This final summation is not present in any of the standard texts.

7

The Army Contending

SUN TZU SAID:

In sum, the method of employing the military—

The general receives the command from the
    sovereign,
Joins with the army, gathers the multitude,
    organizes them and encamps.
Nothing is more difficult than an army contending.

The chain of command is initiated only by the sovereign. The general organizes the army and then takes it into the field. Nothing is more difficult than contending because everything is at stake and so much remains unpredictable.

The difficulty for a contending army
Is to make the circuitous direct
And to make the adverse advantageous.

Thus make their road circuitous
And lure them with advantage.

Setting out later than others and arriving sooner
Is knowing the appraisals of circuitous and direct.

The goal for a contending army is to transform the circuitous and direct. Because the general is not limited by how things are defined for him, he can reverse conditions in various ways, apparently turning logic on its head. He makes the adverse advantageous not by overcoming obstacles but by giving those difficulties to the enemy—making their road circuitous. He offers advantage to confound their perceptions, changing what is easy into what is difficult. Thus he is able to invert space and time, setting out after and arriving before. In these ways he attacks the basic strategy of the enemy.

A contending army brings advantage.
A contending army brings danger.
Contending for advantage with an entire army, one
    will not get there.
Contending for advantage with a reduced army,
    one's baggage train is diminished.

Therefore, rolling up one's armor, hastening after
    advantage day and night without camping,
    continually marching at the double for one
    hundred li and then contending for
    advantage—
  The commander of the three armies is captured.
  The strong ones sooner, the worn-out ones later,
    and one in ten arrives.
Going fifty li and contending for advantage—
  The ranking general falls.
  By this method half arrive.
Going thirty li and contending for advantage—
  Two-thirds arrive.

Therefore—
> An army without a baggage train is lost,
> Without grain and food is lost,
> Without supplies is lost.

Contending is a major function of the military. It cannot be avoided. But rushing to seize advantage on another's ground brings loss of every kind. Keep the army gathered, attending to the basic needs of your troops. Remain with the advantage your current circumstances offer.

Therefore—
> Not knowing the strategies of the feudal lords,
> One cannot ally with them.
> Not knowing the form of mountains and forests,
>   defiles and gorges, marshes and swamps,
> One cannot move the army.
> Not employing local guides,
> One cannot obtain the advantage of the ground.

Without knowledge one cannot act skillfully. Knowledge must come from every available source and extend to all aspects of the enemy.

> And so the military is based on guile,
> Acts due to advantage,
> Transforms by dividing and joining.

The all-victorious military is founded in deception, motivated by victory and endlessly transforming. These are the basic elements of the general's knowledge.

And so—
> Swift like the wind,
> Slow like the forest,
> Raiding and plundering like fire,
> Not moving like a mountain,
> Difficult to know like yin,
> Moving like thunder.

Yin is the mate of yang. It is dark, quiet, hidden.

Six ways of moving. Six ways of being and of changing. These powers of the natural world are the powers of the skillful general, of the victorious military. Who can resist the wind or move a mountain?

> When plundering the countryside, divide the
> multitude.
> When expanding territory, divide the advantage.
> Weigh it and act.

Disperse your troops and distribute the goods among them. By dividing captured resources, one strengthens loyalties. As these resources are balanced throughout one's realm, they become less susceptible to recapture. Thus your actions overlook immediate advantage so as to further victory.

> One who knows in advance the Tao of the
> circuitous and direct is victorious.
> This is the method of the army contending.

The standard text speaks of knowing "the appraisals of the circuitous and direct." Here we follow the bamboo text, which speaks instead of knowing their Tao.

Contending is, finally, a matter of the circuitous and direct. The general knows these in advance, though it is not primarily through information on marshes and swamps or the intent of the feudal lords. Rather it is through an understanding of how things transform and invert: the adverse and advantageous, the circuitous and direct. These are a Tao of the contending army.

Therefore, the *Governance of the Army* says—
    "Because they could not hear each other, they
        made drums and bells.
    Because they could not see each other, they
        made flags and pennants."

Therefore—
    In day battle use more flags and pennants.
    In night battle use more drums and bells.
    Drums and bells, flags and pennants are the means
        by which one unifies the ears and eyes of the
        people.

Once the people have been tightly unified,
The brave have no chance to advance alone,
The cowardly have no chance to retreat alone.
This is the method of employing the many.

The *Governance of the Army* is an otherwise unknown military text. Signals are a solution to military communication in the chaos of movement and battle, in the day or night. Just as signs and symbols foster the coherence of a culture, signals bring unity to the military. They equalize disparities of bravery or cowardice and prevent extreme cases of independent action, even under intense conditions of battle. Thus the army becomes the focused expression of its leader's strategy.

And so the ch'i of the three armies can be seized.
The heart-mind of the commander can be seized.

Therefore, morning ch'i is sharp, midday ch'i is lazy,
    evening ch'i is spent.
Thus one skilled at employing the military
Avoids their sharp ch'i and strikes their lazy and
    spent ch'i.
This is ordering ch'i.

"Ch'i" is the breath, the life force.

The day, the seasons, the enemy's ch'i—all are cycles. The general does not seek to overcome these nor regulate them but to know their nature. Thus he can seize the opportunities they offer. This is ordering ch'i.

Use order to await chaos.
Use stillness to await clamor.
This is ordering the heart-mind.

The Chinese character for *ordering* has the basic sense of regulating or arranging as well as connotations of ruling. You order the heart-mind by remaining in the stillness and order that are already present at the center of all chaos and clamor.

Use the near to await the far.
Use ease to await labor.
Use fullness to await hunger.
This is ordering strength.

It is not necessary to exercise your strength. Instead, rest in your sufficiency.

Do not engage well-ordered pennants.
Do not strike imposing formations.
This is ordering transformation.

Transformation is a matter of dividing or joining your troops and those of the enemy. You order transformation by holding your seat.

In sum, you order by not doing, particularly when the situation is too strong to alter in any other way. Avoid the enemy's sharp ch'i, wait in stillness, rest in your completeness, do not go against their plenitude. Then you strike their spent or lazy ch'i. This is ordering.

––––––––––

And so the method of employing the military—
    Do not face them when they are on a high hill.
    Do not go against them with their back to a
        mound.
    Do not pursue them when they feign defeat.
    Leave a way out for surrounded soldiers. ∽
    Do not block soldiers returning home. ∽
This is the method of employing the many.

The standard text has these lines in different order and contains as well the following:

    Do not attack sharp troops.
    Do not eat soldier bait.
    Do not press exhausted invaders.

In many simple configurations, the enemy harbors a great strength. Here, it is the kind of shih the general himself seeks to develop: back to a mound, troops energized with desperation. Rather than developing still more powerful countermeasures, he cedes ground, allowing shih advantageous to the enemy to spend itself harmlessly. At the right moment, not acting is the most skillful action.

Four hundred sixty-five.

This number appears at the end of the bamboo strip, separated by two horizontal marks from the sentence "This is the method of employing the many." It records the total number of characters in the chapter, perhaps for verification against the original being copied, perhaps for scribal payment. Other chapters probably had similar indications, but those are not preserved.

8

The Nine Transformations

SUN TZU SAID:

In sum, the method of employing the military—

The general receives the command from the
      sovereign,
Joins with the army and gathers the multitude.

Every standard edition of the *Sun Tzu* contains these two lines. They
are identical to the opening phrases of chapter 7 but do not reproduce
that passage in its entirety. They may be traces of a very early stage in
the book's formation, when the place of these sentences had not yet
been determined. Their presence here demonstrates the loose principles by which the *Sun Tzu* is structured.

In spread-out ground do not encamp.
In junction ground join with allies.
In crossing ground do not linger.
In enclosed ground strategize.
In death ground do battle.

Conditions of the ground dictate the actions you can take. Spread-out ground leaves you exposed to attack. Do not encamp here. The shared and ever-changing borders of junction ground require alliances with neighbors. The intense comings and goings of crossing ground make you vulnerable on every side. Hurry through it. Enclosed ground is hard to enter or leave, so you must plan carefully. Death ground is choiceless.

Every activity, in life as in battle, takes place on a certain ground. Every ground suggests the response most appropriate to it.

There are roads one does not follow.
There are armies one does not strike.
There are cities one does not attack.
There are grounds one does not contest.
There are commands of the sovereign one does
       not accept.

It may seem that the military's objective is to overcome all obstacles. But there are some objectives one simply does not pursue. An enemy position may be too powerful. A ruler's orders may not be based on intimate knowledge of conditions.

It is the general's responsibility to know the ground of each situation. As this shifts and changes, he must look freshly at every circumstance and make his decision. The military seeks not conquest but victory.

And so the general who comprehends the
       advantages of the nine transformations
Knows how to employ the military!
The general who does not comprehend the
       advantages of the nine transformations,
Though knowing the form of the ground, is unable
       to obtain the advantages of the ground!

When one orders the military but does not know
    the teachings of the nine transformations,
Though knowing the five advantages, one is unable
    to employ people!

The five advantages are not specified but may refer to the five grounds mentioned near the start of this chapter. The nine transformations are every possible manifestation of things, the general's treasury of knowledge.

The world is in constant change, yet at each moment it appears as a particular quality, form or shih. Knowing these, you can successfully employ the military. Not knowing these, any other knowledge becomes powerless. If you do not also have the ability to transform endlessly, even the advantages of the five grounds become an inferior knowledge that will only restrict you.

———————

Therefore—
    The plans of the wise necessarily include
        advantage and harm.
    They include advantage. Thus one's service can
        be trusted.
    They include harm. Thus adversity can be
        undone.

Therefore—
    Subdue the feudal lords with harm.
    Occupy the feudal lords with tasks.
    Hasten the feudal lords with advantage.

The general's promise and threat include the full range of action. Thus he can control the activities of both allies and enemies.

———————

And so the method of employing the military—
    Do not rely on their not coming.
    Rely on what we await them with.
    Do not rely on their not attacking.
    Rely on how we are unable to be attacked.

Do not base your plans on what the enemy may do. Rely instead on your preparedness. Better, move entirely outside the grasp of their strategy, and you cannot be attacked.

And so for the general there are five dangers—
    Resolved to die, one can be killed.
    Resolved to live, one can be captured.
    Quick to anger, one can be goaded.
    Pure and honest, one can be shamed.
    Loving the people, one can be aggravated.
All five are the excesses of the general,
A calamity in employing the military.

To overturn an army and kill the general,
One must use the five dangers.
One cannot but examine them.

Willing to die for his cause, being pure and honest, loving the people—even virtues become vulnerabilities when taken to an extreme. The general's fixation offers an easy means to turn his energy back upon him. Simply put him into a situation in which his propensities become intensified, and you find victory.

9

Moving the Army

SUN TZU SAID:

In sum, positioning the army and scrutinizing the
enemy—

The chapter addresses each of these two topics in turn. Taking position concerns finding places that maximize your strength. Scrutinizing
the enemy explains how to gain knowledge of your adversary's conditions by examining the phenomenal world. *Scrutinize* is the word used
for traditional physiognomy, the reading of someone's character from
his or her face.

In crossing mountains,
 Hold to the valleys.
 Look out at life ground and take a high position.
 Battle downhill. Do not ascend.
This is positioning the army in mountains.

Mountains are difficult to cross, as they are full of dangerous and
quick-changing shih. Enter only if you can obtain secure ground.

In crossing water,
>>One must distance oneself from it.
>>When the invader approaches across water, do
>>>not meet him in the water.
>>To order a strike when he is half across is
>>>advantageous.
>>When wishing to do battle,
>>Do not go close to the water to meet the invader.
>>Look out at life ground and take a high position.
>>Do not go against the current.
>This is positioning the army by water.

Water makes for slow crossing, and one remains vulnerable for a considerable time. Take advantage of its ability to disorder the enemy's army.

In crossing salt marshes,
>>Be sure to leave quickly. Do not linger.
>>If one encounters an army in the midst of a salt
>>>marsh,
>>Hold to the water grass and keep one's back to
>>>the trees.
>This is positioning the army in salt marshes.

Salt marshes are unpredictable. Ground you might consider unreliable in other settings could be your best defense.

On plains
>>Take a position on level ground.
>>Keep the high to the right and back.
>>In front, death. Behind, life.
>This is positioning the army on plains.

Plains are open and easy, exposed in every direction. Rely on whatever advantages the terrain may offer, keeping the way clear for escape.

All four are the advantages of the army, how the
    Yellow Emperor was victorious over the Four
    Emperors.

In early mythology the Yellow Emperor is the creator of warfare, defeating the emperors of the four directions.[1] Like the Four Emperors, there are four kinds of terrain considered here.

The ground of any situation, whether physical or psychological, has particular characteristics. These suggest certain cautions.

The general's strength is limited. He positions his troops in relation to the terrain, seeking powerful shih that will magnify their force.

In sum, the army likes the high and hates the low,
Values yang and disdains yin,
Sustains life and takes a position in the solid.
This is what is meant by "surely victorious."
The army is without the hundred afflictions.

Yang is light, open, active and forceful. Yin is its complement.

The victorious army retains the advantage of position, maintains its health and remains firmly encamped, drawing strength from the environment.

In hills and dikes, take a position in yang.
Keep them to the right and back.
This is the advantage of the military, the assistance
    of the earth.

By remaining above the enemy, you battle down. This is using the naturally occurring conditions of the ground to protect your forces.

When it has rained upstream, the stream's flow
    intensifies.
Stop fording. Wait for it to calm.

Some conditions take time to run their course before they are favorable to your movement. If you face a surge of enemy force, it may be best to let it subside before acting.

When crossing heavenly ravines, heavenly wells,
    heavenly prisons, heavenly nets, heavenly
    sinkholes and heavenly fissures,
One must quickly leave them. Do not go near.
When I am far from them, the enemy is near them.
When I face them, the enemy has his back to them.

The particulars of these forms of ground are unknown to commentators. The dangers they conceal are clearly unworkable, however great the general. Simply leave them. Take position so that you direct the enemy into them.

When alongside the army are defiles, ponds, reeds,
    small forests and dense vegetation that can
    conceal people,
Search these carefully and repeatedly.
They are where the devious take position.

Confusion, murk and haze—lack of clarity of any kind—are perfect hiding places for the devious, as they interfere with your clear sight.

When the enemy is near and still, he is relying on
     the steep.
When the enemy is far and provokes battle, he
     wishes the other to advance—
He is occupying the level and advantageous.

This chapter has discussed responses to various types of ground. These lines mark a transition into its second part, which addresses scrutiny—reading enemy conditions from evidence in the phenomenal world.

The enemy's positioning reveals their intention. In each case they seek to engage you from configurations of shih that are disadvantageous to you.

Many trees move.
He is approaching.

Many obstacles in thick grass.
He is misleading us.

Birds rise up.
He is concealing himself.

Animals are startled.
He is launching a total assault.

Trees, plants, birds and beasts represent the fourfold division of the Chinese natural world.

Because all its parts are connected, the environment around the enemy contains invaluable messages of their activity. By reading this environment, you are reading their designs.

Dust is high and sharp.
Chariots are approaching.

It is low and wide.
The infantry is approaching.

It is dispersed and wispy.
The firewood gatherers are approaching.

It is scattered here and there.
He is encamping his army.

Even the dust speaks. This is not book knowledge. This is not even knowledge of the extraordinary and orthodox. This is a scout's observations from the field. Since anything that occurs affects everything around it, the smallest phenomenon leads you to the complete view. This is true from scout's knowledge to the general's total vision.

———————

His words are humble and his preparations increase.
He will advance.

His words are strong and his advance is forced.
He will retreat.

Light chariots come out first and take a position on
     the flank.
He is deploying.

He is not in difficulty yet requests peace.
He is strategizing.

They rush out to deploy.
He has set the moment.

Half of them advance.
He is luring you.

Having read the opposing general through his effect on vegetation, animals and dust, now we read him through his words and deeds. But his actions may not directly represent his intentions. Look for contradictions between the two.

They lean on their weapons.
They are hungry.

Those who draw water drink first.
They are thirsty.

They see advantage but do not advance.
They are tired.

These are indications of increasing devastation. First come signs of hunger, thirst, tiredness—exhaustion of the body. They are apparent as soon as military decorum and procedures are not followed. Thus the importance of maintaining the orthodox, and of noting the enemy's apparently trivial deviations from it.

Birds gather.
It is empty.

They call out at night.
They are afraid.

The encampment is disorderly.
The general has no weight.

Flags and pennants are moved about.
There is chaos.

Officers are angry.
They are fatigued.

They feed grain to their horses and eat meat, the
    army does not hang up their water pots, and
    they do not return to their quarters.
The invaders are exhausted.

Next are signs of disorder in the encampment, which reach an
extreme in frenzied consumption. All regulations governing conduct
and supplies are abandoned.

———————

He repeatedly and soothingly speaks to his men in
    measured tones.
He has lost the multitude.

There are many rewards.
He is in distress.

There are many punishments.
He is in difficulty.

At first he is harsh and later fears the multitude.
He is utterly unskillful.

He approaches with gifts and entreaties.
He wishes to rest.

The military is wrathful and faces one for a long
    time without either engaging or withdrawing.
One must carefully examine this.

Finally we examine the enemy general's state of mind. As he is key to uniting the army, his methods of command immediately reveal conditions within his military. Here he has lost the Tao of leadership.

By its very unpredictability, such an army can cause considerable damage. If its intentions are not fully apparent, be wary.

In the military more is not better.

Do not advance in a martial way.
It is sufficient to gather strength, assess the enemy
    and take him—that is all.

However, if one does not plan and takes the enemy
    lightly,
One will certainly be captured by him.

Victory arises from preponderance, which grows from knowledge and is expressed in mastery of shih. Do not seek it in accumulation alone.

Do not waste resources in military display. The moment advantageous conditions arise, recognize them and direct your forces there. Swift victory is the general's goal.

If the troops do not yet feel close kinship with one
    and they are punished, they will not submit.
If they do not submit, they are difficult to employ.
If the troops already feel close kinship with one and
    punishments are not carried out, do not
    employ them.

The general establishes close kinship with those in his command. Thus troops can execute their duties even under the most difficult conditions. Without bonds of loyalty, punishment is felt only as pain and causes resentment. With kinship established, punishment is understood as a matter of taking responsibility for one's actions. Then it expresses what is right and true. It must be carried out to maintain the integrity of this military world.

> And so assemble them by fellowship,
> Make them uniform by the martial.
> This is what is meant by "certain to seize it."

In assembling an army, individuals are brought into association from many conditions. They become soldiers only when the general unites them. He creates such powerful bonds that all come to share the same intentions. Transformed by discipline and care, they can undertake their dangerous tasks together.

> If one acts consistently to train the people, the
>   people will submit.
> If one acts inconsistently to train the people, the
>   people will not submit.
> One who acts consistently is in accord with the
>   multitude.

"One who acts consistently is in accord with the multitude." Literally the text says that the general and his army "gain each other." Thus the troops "can die with him, live with him and not deceive him" (chapter 1).

Consistent leadership allows people to develop confidence that their environment is intact and trustworthy, worth exerting themselves for. Otherwise, not knowing what to expect, they cannot relax into their world and fully assume their roles.

IO

Forms of the Earth

SUN TZU SAID:

The forms of the earth—
   open, hung, stalled, narrow, steep and distant.

Although terrain is also discussed in other parts of the text, these six forms of earth are unique to this chapter. They are not only physical shape and dimension but equally the qualities of ground and the kinds of interaction that can take place upon it.

———————

I am able to go. He is able to come. This is called
   "open."
As for the open form—
   Be first to occupy the high and yang.
   Secure your supply routes.
   If I do battle, it is advantageous.

The open form refers to any space where you and the other can move freely in and out. Since it is equally available to both, you must be first to establish a strong position there.

I can go but it is difficult to return. This is called
     "hung."
As for the hung form—
     When the enemy is unprepared, I emerge and
          am victorious over him.
     When the enemy is prepared, if I emerge and am
          not victorious,
     It is difficult to return.
     It is not advantageous.

Once this space has been entered, no one can move cleanly out.
Whoever tries to do so will be snagged by some obstacle. Thus take
action only if you are certain it will lead to victory.

I emerge and it is not advantageous. He emerges
     and it is not advantageous. This is called
     "stalled."
As for the stalled form—
     Although the enemy offers me advantage, I do
          not emerge. I lead my troops away.
     To order a strike when half the enemy has
          emerged is advantageous.

The stalled form offers no ready advantage. Enter only when the
enemy have exposed their vulnerability.

As for the narrow form—
     If I occupy it first, I must fill it and await the
          enemy.

If the enemy occupies it first and fills it, do not
  pursue.
If he does not fill it, pursue.

The narrow form becomes advantageous only if you occupy it completely. Then there are no options left to the enemy.

———————

As for the steep form—
If I occupy it first, I must occupy the high and
  yang and await the enemy.
If the enemy occupies it first, I lead the troops away.
Do not pursue.

Great promise of advantage, great danger. If you cannot secure its
benefits, avoid this form of the earth.

———————

As for the distant form—
Since shih is equal, it is difficult to provoke battle.
To do battle is not advantageous.

There is no way to engage the enemy. You can offer no apparent
advantage to draw them out, there is no clear way in, and you have no
obvious preponderance.

———————

All these six are a Tao of the earth,
The general's utmost responsibility.
One cannot but examine them.

The earth—or the ground of any situation—offers certain conditions
within which battle can take place. One must respect these conditions
and follow the actions they dictate. They cannot be manipulated.

The ground of conflict is shared, and these six forms of the earth belong to no one. Their shih change constantly as we move through them. Thus the narrow can become the steep, which can become the distant. These forms of shih can be discerned in any situation.

These are called a Tao of the earth, standing for the countless ways the earth takes form and human beings join with it to form shih. It is the general's responsibility to know them all. This is not done by knowing just these six, nor by knowing every possible one, but by seeing how this knowledge forms a whole.

> And so in the military there is driven off, the bow
>   unstrung, dragged down, the mountain
>   collapsing, chaos and routed.
> All these six are not a calamity of heaven.
> They are the excesses of the general.

Battle occurs in a particular ground, but it is the general who determines what takes place there. If he does not fulfill his proper role, he brings heavenlike calamity upon his forces.

> Now shih is equal and he uses one to strike ten.
> This is called "driven off."

Two forces have equal advantage of the earth. If the general sets his smaller force against the enemy's larger, he will be put to flight.

> The troops are strong and the officers weak.
> This is called "the bow unstrung."

Strong forces without leadership are a weapon without a trigger.

The officers are strong and the troops weak.
This is called "dragged down."

Even the strongest officers cannot hold up weak troops.

A great officer is wrathful and does not submit.
When he encounters the enemy,
He is filled with rancor and does battle on his own.
The general does not know his ability.
This is called "the mountain collapsing."

An officer's fierce wrath turns to rage in the face of battle, bringing down the army with him. His general had no knowledge of this propensity.

The general is weak and not strict.
His training and leadership are not clear.
The officers and troops are inconstant.
The formations of the military are jumbled.
This is called "chaos."

When the general does not lead, the army cannot follow. All becomes confusion.

The general cannot assess the enemy.
With the few he engages the many.
With the weak he strikes the strong.
The military is without elite forces.
This is called "routed."

Without knowledge of the enemy, the general commits catastrophic errors. All is lost.

All these six are a Tao of defeat,
The general's utmost responsibility.
One cannot but examine them.

Like the forms of earth, these six are a Tao. Taken as a whole, they represent the multiplicity of ways in which the general will be defeated before battle ever takes place. He must know the dangers of them all.

Now forms of the earth are an assistance to the
      military.
Assess the enemy and determine victory.
Appraise the steep and level, the far and near.
This is a Tao of the superior general.
One who knows these and employs battle is
      certainly victorious.
One who does not know these and employs battle is
      certainly defeated.

These are three kinds of knowledge that the general possesses. He discerns the true forms of earth, and their assistance arises naturally for him. He sees the strength and weakness of his enemy and their leadership. He can read the shih of varied landscapes and circumstances. Knowing these as a Tao brings victory.

And so when according to the Tao of battle there is
      certain victory and the ruler says do not do
      battle, one can certainly do battle.

When according to the Tao of battle there is no
     victory and the ruler says one must do battle,
     one can not do battle.

The sovereign chooses the general for his ability to attain victory.
Final judgment about doing battle is the general's responsibility alone.
That determination arises from his full knowledge of battleground conditions, where advantage constantly transforms and shifts. Respecting
the ruler's confidence, discerning the present moment and trusting his
judgment, the general finds victory.

And so he advances yet does not seek fame.
He retreats yet does not avoid blame.
He seeks only to preserve the people,
And his advantage accords with that of the ruler.
He is the treasure of the state.

The general remains attuned to the vision of the sovereign and the
welfare of the people. Thus he is not confused by praise, blame or reputation. As nothing can prevent him from proper action, he keeps to
victory by taking whole.

He looks upon the troops as his children.
Thus they can venture into deep river valleys with him.
He looks upon the troops as his beloved sons.
Thus they can die together with him.

United in profound kinship with their general, the troops respond
with uncompromising loyalty. They will obey every order. They will
accompany him anywhere, into grave danger, into death.

He is generous yet unable to lead.
He is loving yet unable to give orders.
He is chaotic and unable to bring order.
They are like spoiled children.
They cannot be employed.

By themselves, virtues such as kindness or love are ineffective means of leadership. They must be fully joined to clear discipline before they foster a natural hierarchy of things. The general must be soft and hard, a proper yes and a proper no. Only then can his army arise in order.

Knowing my troops can strike, yet not knowing the
        enemy cannot be struck.
This is half of victory.

Knowing the enemy can be struck, yet not knowing
        my soldiers cannot strike.
This is half of victory.

Knowing the enemy can be struck, knowing my
        soldiers can strike, yet not knowing that the
        form of the earth cannot be used to do battle.
This is half of victory.

This is the initial summary of the chapter.
Knowledge of self and other is vital to the general in every endeavor. Yet it is insufficient without knowledge of the ground, the environment within which battle occurs.

And so one who knows the military
Acts and is not confused,
Initiates and is not exhausted.

This is the second summary of the chapter.

The general is clear-minded and inexhaustible. His clarity arises from his intimate knowledge of the military, and thus his actions lead to victory even in conditions of chaos. He is not depleted because he gains energy by moving with the forms of earth, the larger patterns of his world.

And so it is said—
    Know the other and know oneself, ～
    Then victory is not in danger. ～
    Know earth and know heaven, ～
    Then victory can be complete. ～

In ancient China "heaven" stands for the range of phenomena from weather to celestial process to the imperial vision. "Earth" extends similarly from terrain to the practical grounds of any activity.

Danger can be avoided by knowing self and other. Being all-victorious depends on knowledge of heaven and earth.

11

The Nine Grounds

SUN TZU SAID:

The method of employing the military—

This chapter speaks to a multitude of military methods. The first two-thirds addresses the nine grounds and command of troops within enemy territory. Then the nine grounds are discussed again, and the chapter turns to general military matters.

There is dispersed ground, light ground, contested
  ground, connected ground, junction ground,
  heavy ground, spread-out ground, enclosed
  ground and death ground.

The feudal lords battle for this ground.
This is "dispersed."

All parties consider this ground important, and there are no means to gain easy advantage. Do not fight over it.

I enter another's ground, but not deeply.
This is "light."

Do not engage or make a commitment here. The shih is not yet favorable.

If I obtain it, it is advantageous. If he obtains it, it
    is also advantageous.
This is "contested."

Since anyone can benefit from possessing this ground, your enemy will surely want it. Prevent this. Use care in initiating an attack.

I am able to go. He is able to come.
This is "connected."

Because this ground is equally available to all, everyone is vulnerable. Cross only if you are well protected. Establish ties where it is possible.

Where the grounds of three feudal lords meet, the
    one who arrives first will obtain the multi-
    tudes of all-under-heaven.
This is "junction."

This boundary is shared, and each of the three parties has a home base nearby. If you are first to establish yourself strongly, you can dominate all. This will require allegiances.

I enter another's ground deeply, with many walled
    cities and towns at my back.
This is "heavy."

Since you are deeply committed, keep your forces tightly gathered.
With no possibility of support from home, you must be self-sufficient.

———————

I move through mountains, forests and swamps—in
    sum, roads difficult to move along.
This is "spread-out."

In such places it is easy for the enemy to establish threatening positions. Do not linger.

———————

The way by which I exit and enter is narrow.
The way by which I pursue and return is circuitous.
His few can strike my many.
This is "enclosed."

With access limited and pathways indirect, this ground promises great danger. All forms of shih work in the enemy's favor. You must block his access to them. Only careful planning will see you out.

———————

If quick, I survive.
If not quick, I am lost.
This is "death."

No choice but to do battle. Everything will be won with swift action, or lost without it.

Therefore—
    In dispersed ground do not do battle.
    In light ground do not stop.
    In contested ground do not attack.
    In connected ground do not cross.
    In junction ground join with allies.
    In heavy ground plunder.
    In spread-out ground move.
    In enclosed ground strategize.
    In death ground do battle.

Four of these nine grounds are discussed at the beginning of chapter 8. All nine also appear again in the middle of this chapter.

This passage demonstrates the great utility of naming. Nine times it captures a complex relationship in a phrase or two, such as "I am able to go. He is able to come." Then it reduces that to a single word: "This is 'connected.'" In conclusion, it offers pith advice: "In connected ground do not cross."

Once you have the name, you have captured the essence, and your more complete knowledge of the situation readily arises. Then it is easy to see the great variety of responses that may be called for. These nine are not exhaustive. Instead they urge us to build our repertory of understanding, to begin to master all possibilities that may arise.

In ancient times those called skilled at battle were
    able to prevent—
    The enemy's van and rear from reaching each
      other, ～
    The many and the few from relying on each
      other, ～
    Noble and base from helping each other, ～
    Superior and inferior from coordinating with
      each other, ～

Separated troops from regrouping, ∾
The assembled military from becoming uniform. ∾

Separate that which holds the other together—kinship, alliances, coordination, the root of their strength. When that unity is cut, what was a single Tao becomes many parts. Thus one skilled in battle cuts down the enemy's strategy.

If it accords with advantage, then act.
If it does not accord with advantage, then stop.

Advantage is anything that brings victory. For the sage commander, there is no other motivation to action.

Dare one ask,
    "The enemy, amassed and in good order, is about
        to approach.
    How do I await him?"
I say,
    "Seize what he loves, and he will heed you!"

Do not confront the enemy in their strength, but seize something they hold dear. Their force is useless here; they must stop to listen. You need not destroy the enemy's cherished object or their forces. Instead you can take them whole.

Anything you cherish makes you vulnerable. Prepare yourself to relinquish it.

It is the nature of the military that swiftness rules.
Ride others' inadequacies.

Go by unexpected ways.
Attack where he has not taken precautions.

Attack swiftly where the enemy is weak, where they are not, where they are undefended. These are the empty. Your momentum only increases because they offer no resistance. These are means of skillful movement.

In sum, the Tao of being an invader—

Enter deeply and one is concentrated.
The defenders do not subdue one. ~

Plunder rich countryside.
The three armies have enough to eat. ~

Carefully nourish and do not work them.
Consolidate ch'i and accumulate strength. ~

Move the military about and appraise one's
strategies.
Be unfathomable. ~

Hostile ground heightens your focus. Cut off from home support, you take nourishment from the enemy. Such supply lines cannot be severed. Use the threat surrounding you to stay gathered and sustain your troops. Varying your form, plans, location and intention, you cannot be known.

Throw them where they cannot leave.
Facing death, they will not be routed. ~
Officers and men facing death, ~
How could one not obtain their utmost strength? ~

When military officers are utterly sinking, they do
not fear. ~

Where they cannot leave, they stand firm. ～
When they enter deep, they hold tightly. ～
Where they cannot leave, they fight. ～

Therefore, they are—
    Untuned yet disciplined, ～
    Unsought yet obtained, ～
    Without covenant yet in kinship,
    Without orders yet trusting. ～

Extreme situations cause your troops to respond from profound sources of power. Training and commands cannot accomplish this. Dire configurations of shih, however, automatically evoke it. It is unsought, yet attained.

Prohibit omens, remove doubt, and even death
        seems no disaster.

When soldiers face death, the structures of military life become irrelevant. In such extreme conditions, one can let go of omens or doubts—the mirage of mysterious forces and second thoughts. As smaller reference points dissolve, everything turns clear and immediate. Even death—the ultimate point of reference—has no special power.

My officers do not have surplus wealth.
It is not that they hate goods.
They do not have surplus deaths.
It is not that they hate longevity.

On the day that orders are issued,
The tears of seated officers moisten their lapels,
The tears of those reclining cross their cheeks.

Throw them where they cannot leave—
It is the bravery of Chuan Chu and Ts'ao Kuei.

Chuan Chu and Ts'ao Kuei were military retainers known for acts of outrageous courage. Their tales, from the sixth and seventh centuries BCE, are recounted in the *Historical Records*.[1]

Your troops are ordinary human beings. They love goods and hate death. They can be overcome by their emotions. Such attributes might call into question their appropriateness for military service. But these qualities are what make them effective soldiers. Bravery arises from cowardice. Threatened with loss of life, they fight desperately to survive. Placed in the right shih, their natural response unleashes enormous power.

———————

And so one skilled at employing the army may be
        compared to the shuai-jan.
The shuai-jan is a snake of Mount Heng.
Strike its head and the tail arrives.
Strike its tail and the head arrives.
Strike its midsection and both head and tail arrive.

Dare one ask,
    "Can one then make them like the shuai-jan?"
I reply,
    "One can. The people of Yueh and the people of
        Wu hate each other.
    When they are in the same boat crossing the river,
    They help each other like the left and right hand."

Though there are various accounts of the shuai-jan in Chinese mythology, this is the earliest recorded reference to it.

Yueh and Wu were bitter rivals in the sixth century BCE. Sun Tzu is said to have assisted the ruler of Wu in his defeat of Yueh, though his name does not appear in the historical records of that conflict.

The shuai-jan is perfectly coordinated with itself. It is instinctively of one mind. In the right conditions, even otherwise opposing elements join as one body. Here those conditions are the threat of death, which evokes powers comparable to those of the mythic world.

―――――――

Therefore, tying horses together and burying wheels
Is not enough to rely on.

Make bravery uniform.
This is a Tao of governance.

Attain both hard and soft.
This is a pattern of earth.

The Chinese word for *governance* implies "correcting" or "making orthodox."

Placing physical objects between you and the enemy will not defend you from their attack. Instead transform your soldiers. Find shih that unifies them in mind, so that extremes of cowardice or bravery are moderated. This is skill in ordering.

At the same time, master the natural world. Hard and soft are forms of earth and also the qualities of any situation. To take it whole, you must be able to hold all possibilities and extremes.

―――――――

And so one skilled at employing the military takes
them by the hand as if leading a single
person.
They cannot hold back.

Your command is so intimate, the troops hear you as if you were speaking singly to each of them. United in this kinship, they cannot but follow you.

In his activity ～
The commander is tranquil and thus inscrutable,
Orthodox and thus brings order. ～
He is able to stupefy the ears and eyes of officers
        and troops,
Preventing them from having it. ～

He changes his activities, ～
Alters his strategies,
Preventing the people from discerning. ～

He changes his camp, ～
Makes his route circuitous, ～
Preventing the people from obtaining his plans. ～

To be invisible, you must first be so orthodox that nothing remains to give you away. Then you must be so extraordinary that no one can predict your location or purpose.

You must be equally ungraspable to your own troops. This is for their safety as well as the authority of your command.

The leader sets the time of battle with them, ～
Like climbing high and removing the ladder. ～
The leader enters with them deep into the land of
        the feudal lords, ～
Pulling the trigger. ～

Like driving a flock of sheep,
He drives them there,
He drives them here, ～
No one knows where they are going. ～

He gathers the multitude of the three armies
And throws them into the defile.

This is what is meant by "the activity of the
    commander."

The general is responsible for victory. Thus he throws his troops
into circumstances that realize their greatest strength, setting the
moment of its release. They must be allowed no knowledge of these
conditions. They can have no choice but to follow him. In times of
extreme peril, such decisive action is not only effective, it may be one's
only means of survival. Success depends on the troops' utter loyalty.

The variations of the nine grounds,
The advantages of contracting and extending,
The pattern of human nature—
One cannot but examine them.

Here the chapter is summarized in terms of its three major themes,
which are three kinds of knowledge the general must possess. First are
the nine grounds—forms of shih and the advantage that comes from
each. Second are principles of movement, either withdrawing from
the enemy or expanding one's position. Third is knowing human
nature, which allows the general to predict troops' reactions to varied
circumstances.

The chapter then begins again, reintroducing the nine grounds and
moving to general military matters.

In sum, being an invader—
    Deep then concentrated,
    Shallow then dispersed.

To leave the state and go over the border with
    soldiers. This is crossing ground.

Four ways in. This is junction ground.

To enter deeply. This is heavy ground.

To enter shallowly. This is light ground.

Unyielding at the back, narrow in front. This is
enclosed ground.

Unyielding at the back, enemy in front. This is
death ground.

No way to leave. This is exhaustion ground.

This initial set of seven grounds includes "exhaustion ground," which is found only in the bamboo text. Of these seven, five are included among the following set of nine.

————————

Therefore—

In dispersed ground I will unify their will.

In light ground I will make them come together.

In contested ground I will keep them from
lingering.

In connected ground I will make firm my ties.

In junction ground I will be careful of what I
rely on.

In heavy ground I will hasten to bring up my rear.

In spread-out ground I will advance along his
roads.

In enclosed ground I will block the gaps.

In death ground I will show them that we will
not live.

These nine grounds are identical to those presented at the start of this chapter. The pith instructions from that section are rendered here with somewhat varied emphases.

And so the nature of the feudal lords—
    When enclosed, they resist.
    When there is no holding back, they fight.
    When overcome, they follow.

Creating barriers intensifies the space that they enclose. The enemy hardens their position. When all alternatives are closed off, the enemy's resistance turns into battle. Then they will go along with you only after having been thoroughly overcome.

Therefore—
    Not knowing the strategies of the feudal lords,
    One cannot ally with them.
    Not knowing the form of mountains and forests,
        defiles and gorges, marshes and swamps,
    One cannot move the army.
    Not employing local guides,
    One cannot obtain the advantage of the ground.
    Not knowing one of these four or five,
    One is not the military of the kings and
        overlords.

"Kings" were the rulers of states in the fourth and third centuries BCE. "Overlord" was the title of several rulers who briefly established hegemony over the others. The first six lines appear verbatim in chapter 7, suggesting that this part of the chapter is especially loose in organization.

The passage reiterates the importance of knowledge to any form of action. The final two lines, however, show that it is necessary to possess *all* these types of knowledge, transforming this section from a list of observations to a list of essentials.

The military of those kings and overlords—
>If they attack a great state, then its multitude is
>>unable to gather together.
>Their awesomeness spreads over the enemy, and
>>his allies cannot assemble.

Therefore—
>Do not contend for allies in all-under-heaven.
>Do not cultivate balance in all-under-heaven.
>Trust in self-interest.
>Spread one's awesomeness over the enemy.
Thus his state can be seized and his walled cities
>can be made to submit.

Your great power prevents the enemy from forming a cohesive unit
or joining with their peers. Thus you attack their alliances.

The overlords obtained hegemony through the careful balancing
of allies and enemies. Work instead from your own power to overawe,
drawing the other fully into your world. This is victory, which comes
always from the larger reference point.

>Without method's rewards, ∾
>Without proper orders, ∾
>Bind the multitude of the three armies ∾
>As if leading a single person. ∾

>Bind them with deeds. Do not command them with
>>words.
>Bind them with harm. Do not command them with
>>advantage.

>Mire them in the ground of extinction and still
>>they survive.
>Sink them in death ground and still they live.

Now the multitude is sunk in harm, ∼
Yet still they are able to make defeat into victory. ∼

Without resort to hope and fear, consistency or kindness, discarding all conventions of leadership, the general binds the troops to him. He relies not on words but on action that cuts to the bone, bypassing concept and kindness. Thrown into the certainty of death, his troops transform hopelessness into victory.

———————————

And so conducting the affairs of the military ∼
Lies in carefully discerning the enemy's purpose. ∼
Concentrate strength in one direction. ∼
Go one thousand li and kill his general. ∼
This is what is meant by "skillful deeds."

If you know the enemy's purpose, you can find their vital point. Focus your energy there, and strike. Thus you can end the conflict with a single blow, even from a great distance. You need not destroy their goods or people. This is taking whole.

———————————

Therefore, on the day the policy is initiated— ∼
Close the passes and break the tallies.
Do not let their emissaries pass. ∼
Hone it in the upper court
In order to fix the matter. ∼

In ancient China a messenger from the field proved his genuineness by producing the other half of a wooden tally, which had previously been split between commander and sovereign. Here all tallies are destroyed.

The moment war is declared, abruptly change the protocols of diplomatic relations. Secure your boundaries and plan at the highest level.

When the enemy opens the outer gate, ～
One must quickly enter. ～
Make what he loves the first objective.
Hide the time of battle from him. ～
Discard the ink line and respond to the enemy ～
In order to decide the matter of battle. ～

Therefore—
    At first be like a virgin. ～
    The enemy opens the door. ～
    Afterward be like an escaped rabbit. ～
    The enemy will be unable to resist. ～

The ink line is the equivalent of the carpenter's chalk line. It is snapped to ensure that marks are drawn straight.

When obstacles disappear during battle, move quickly to seize the crucial goal. Prevent the enemy from reestablishing equilibrium. At this point you must discard the even measures that have been essential to your process so far and respond to whatever form the enemy offers. Just as water determines its movement in accordance with the ground, the military determines victory in accordance with the enemy.

Innocence disarms. Swiftness is victorious.

12

Attack by Fire

SUN TZU SAID:

In sum, there are five attacks by fire—
    The first is called "setting fire to people."
    The second is called "setting fire to stores."
    The third is called "setting fire to baggage
        trains."
    The fourth is called "setting fire to armories."
    The fifth is called "setting fire in tunnels."

In ancient China siege parties sometimes tunneled under city walls. One means of defense was to pump poisonous gas into the invaders' tunnel.[1]

Modern warfare can be considered the age of fire, as it depends on technologies that range from gunpowder to thermonuclear weapons.[2] Though the scale in this chapter is much smaller, the principle is the same.

Fire consumes and devastates. It is a primordial element, immediately directing the enemy's attention to the most critical factors. Thus its power to abruptly transform a situation is greater than other forms of direct attack.

Making fire has requisites.
The requisites must be sought out and prepared.

There is a season for setting fires.
There are days for starting fires.
The season is when heaven is dry.
The days are when the lunar mansion is the
        Winnowing Basket, the Wall, the Wings, and
        the Chariot Platform.
All four lunar mansions are days when the wind rises.

The Chinese divided the celestial sphere into twenty-eight equal sections, "like segments of an orange."[3] These are the lunar mansions, named for the constellation at the horizon that marks each segment.

Heaven and earth set forth the conditions in which fire can be employed. The earth provides the materials necessary for fire building, and heaven periodically offers the optimum meteorological conditions. Employ fire only when events support it and conditions are auspicious.

If fire is set inside, respond immediately from the
        outside.
If fire is set and his military is still, do not attack.
Rush to where the fire is calamitous.
If one can pursue them, then pursue.
If one cannot pursue, then stop.

If fire can be set outside, do not wait to set it inside.
Set it according to the season.

Go to the point of greatest calamity. Don't assume fire has made the enemy vulnerable. Keep your energy gathered and move only to take advantage of their confusion.

Since it is easier to set a fire on the outside of the enemy's protected space, do so if the opportunity arises.

If fire is set upwind, do not attack from downwind.
If during the day wind is prolonged, at night the
  wind will stop.
One must know the variations of the five fires.
Use counting to watch for the time.

"Counting" refers to the calculations—astronomical and calendrical—by which one determines the proper time for fire making.

As with any natural force, fire's powers are subtle, varied and intense. The general must know the basic types and their innumerable variations. This requires the ability to discern natural patterns, on both a small and large scale.

And so one who uses fire to aid an attack is
  dominant. ∼
One who uses water to aid an attack is strong. ∼
Water can be used to cut off. ∼
It cannot be used to seize. ∼

"Water can be used to cut off." The reference is to events like the diversion of the river Chin, used to surround and flood the city Chin-yang in the fifth century BCE. The siege is said to have lasted three years.[4]

Water can strengthen you, but using fire is an outrageous act, to which the enemy cannot but respond. It can bring closure to a campaign.

Now battle for victory, attack and attain it.
But if one does not follow up on the achievement,
  it is inauspicious.
One's fate is "wealth flowing away."

Thus it is said—
> The enlightened ruler contemplates it.
> The good general follows up on it.

When you have committed to extreme action, be prepared to take advantage of the chaotic conditions you create. Winning on the battlefield is an initial step toward victory. Unless you can extend this achievement, its value is lost. This depends both on the enlightened ruler's vision and on his general's ability to bring it to fruition.

> If it is not advantageous, do not act.
> If it is not attainable, do not employ troops.
> If it is not in danger, do not do battle.

Victory is the general's goal. Do not engage in military activity if no benefit will accrue from it.

> The ruler cannot raise an army on account of wrath.
> The general cannot do battle on account of rancor.
> If it accords with advantage, then employ troops.
> If it does not, then stop.

> Wrath can return to joy.
> Rancor can return to delight.
> An extinguished state cannot return to existence.
> The dead cannot return to life.
> Thus the enlightened sovereign is careful about this.
> The good general is cautious about this.

> These are a Tao of securing the state and keeping
> the army whole.

The nature of most polarities is that they are reversible. These include like and dislike or the extraordinary and orthodox, which turn quickly each into the other. Life and death succeed each other, like the waxing and waning moon. But human dead do not come back to life, nor does the extinguished state return to protect its people.

Attack by fire, and other unremitting applications of force, cause irreversible destruction to every part of life. If loosed in wrath, the opportunity for advantage is lost as well. Since his objective is to safeguard state and army, the general must use them only as part of taking whole.

13

Employing Spies

SUN TZU SAID:

In sum—
When raising one hundred thousand soldiers and
        setting out on a campaign of one thousand li,
        the expenses of the hundred clans and the
        contributions of the nation are one thousand
        gold pieces a day.
Inner and outer are disturbed.
People are exhausted on the roads.
Seven hundred thousand households are unable to
        manage their affairs.

Virtually all these phrases are also found in chapter 2's critique of
the costs of war. They demonstrate the way this text is assembled from
a pool of shared terms and concepts.

Responding to conflict with massed aggression is severely damaging
to one's world—from immediate concerns to international relations.

———————

On guard against them for years to contend for a
      single day's victory, yet, by begrudging rank
      and the reward of a hundred gold pieces, he
      does not know the nature of the enemy.
He is utterly inhumane.
He is not the general of the people.
He is not the assistant of the ruler.
He is not the ruler of victory.

Each day the army is in the field costs one thousand gold pieces. Yet real knowledge of the enemy can give you victory in a day. Such knowledge can only be obtained through spies.

The general may be reluctant to employ spies. He must honor them with the same reward and rank as his bravest soldiers. This may seem like compromising the integrity of the military. Yet in adopting that view, he prolongs the destruction of human life, undermines his sovereign's power and fails to attain victory.

When the general knows taking whole, deception can be a part of genuineness.

And so the means by which an enlightened
      sovereign and a wise general act, and so are
      victorious over others and achieve merit
      superior to the multitude's—
This is foreknowledge.

    Foreknowledge cannot be grasped from ghosts
      and spirits,
    Cannot be inferred from events,
    Cannot be projected from calculation.
    It must be grasped from people's knowledge.

Knowledge leads to victory. Spies lead to knowledge. The general seeks insight into the enemy's processes and procedures from the inside out. The goal is not merely advance warning but understanding how something set in motion will turn out.

Foreknowledge is especially difficult to obtain, since it concerns things that no one can see. Spirit divination presupposes a hidden reality with power over events. Inference assumes that precedents will hold good into the future. Extrapolation is distanced from the intimate situation of here and now. Each has its use, but one can be sure about the future only through knowledge that is immediate, concrete, detailed and complex in human ways. Its best source is direct perception.

And so there are five kinds of spy to employ.
There is the native spy, the inner spy, the turned
    spy, the dead spy and the living spy.
When the five spies arise together and no one
    knows their Tao,
This is what is meant by "spiritlike web."
It is the treasure of the people's sovereign.

The living spy returns and reports.
Employ the native spy from among the local people.
Employ the inner spy from among their officials.
Employ the turned spy from among enemy spies.
The dead spy spreads false information abroad.
    I order my spy to know it, and he transmits
    it to the enemy spy.

Your spies come from every part of society, bringing knowledge of the full range of enemy life. When their activities are woven together, they become an elusive network that is everywhere at once. No one knows where they might appear. They are a great treasury of knowledge.

And so, in the kinship of the three armies—
No kinship is more intimate than that of a spy.
No reward is more generous than that for a spy.
No affair is more secret than that of a spy.

If not a sage, one cannot employ spies.
If not humane, one cannot send out spies.
If not subtle and secret, one cannot obtain a spy's
treasure.

Secret! Secret!
There is nothing for which one cannot employ spies.

When the affairs of a spy are heard before they are
under way,
The spy and those who have been told all die.

The standard text has "If one is not humane and righteous," citing the paramount virtues of Confucianism. The bamboo text has only "humane," which, in its non-Confucian use, means kindly or generous. Later editors apparently tried to bring the *Sun Tzu* under Confucian sway.

A sage is the highest wisdom holder in the Chinese world. His supreme qualities of mind give him the ability to shape the present and know the future.

The spy is an authentic source of knowledge that must be cherished, nurtured and rewarded. In this relationship everything is intensified: the kinship, the potential for new knowledge, the consequences. This weapon is so sharp that it must be kept concealed. Otherwise it may unpredictably injure itself or you. This has its own rules.

One must be a sage to use spies, to feel their vulnerability, to keep oneself and them from jeopardy, to manage the delicacy of their operations amid the enemy, to interpret and apply their knowledge, to handle reversals and false information. Things can go quickly and disastrously wrong.

In sum,
The army one wishes to strike, the walled city one
        wishes to attack and the person one wishes to
        kill—
One must first know the family name and given
        name of the defending general, his intimates,
        the steward, the gatekeeper and attendants.
I order my spy to surely seek them out and know
        them.

The more extreme your action, the more detailed your foreknowledge must be.

I must seek out the enemy's spies who come to spy
        on me.
Accordingly, I benefit them, direct them and then
        release them.
Thus a turned spy can be obtained and employed.

With this knowledge the local spy and the inner
        spy can thus be obtained and sent out.
With this knowledge the dead spy thus spreads false
        information and can be sent to tell the enemy.
With this knowledge the living spy can thus be sent
        out on time.

One must know the matter of the five spies.
Knowing it surely lies in the turned spy.
Thus one cannot but be generous with a turned spy.

Knowledge from the turned spy is a foundation for all the general's action. Even more than a captured charioteer, he must be rewarded and brought around. Through him the general may learn the intentions behind enemy action. Thus he can direct the activities of all other spies, defeating the enemy by "cutting down their strategy."

Directing the turned spy requires particular attention. He has already once betrayed his lord, and he may betray you as well. You must be most intimate with him.

In usual circumstances, the general holds firm the boundaries. Here he is sending people behind enemy borders and welcoming others within his own. The general, then, must be able to maintain or cross boundaries without regard to how others see them. He is beyond predictability, holding a vision that is invisible until the result shows victory.

Like forms of esoteric knowledge, spying can be dangerous, unappealing, shifty and profound. It must be kept secret.

When Yin arose, I Chih was in Hsia.
When Chou arose, Lü Ya was in Yin.

According to legend, I Chih and Lü Ya were noble ministers who betrayed their evil rulers to virtuous invaders. The *Sun Tzu* is arguing that these men of highest reputation were in fact "turned spies." This interpretation has not been accepted by later Confucian readers.

The preceding two lines are from the received text. The bamboo text is fragmentary here but adds the following: "When Yen arose, Su Ch'in was in Ch'i." The figure of Su Ch'in appears in legends of persuasion and betrayal from the years around 300 BCE.

Tradition made Sun Tzu a contemporary of Confucius (551–479), but most scholars now date the principal assemblage of his lineage text to sometime in the fourth century BCE. The presence of someone like Su Ch'in implies either a later date for its compilation, the continuing permeability of its boundaries after the mid-300s or both.

Only if the enlightened ruler and wise general can
    use people of superior knowledge as spies will
    they surely achieve great merit.

These are essentials of the military.
The three armies rely on them and act.

Superior knowledge is difficult to attain. It depends on people like
I Chih or Lü Ya, who can keep their competing alliances separate and
maintain the consistency of their disparate realms.

Knowledge is the basis for any action. Superior knowledge will
assure victory.

About the Translation

OUR TRANSLATION SEEKS TO MAKE THE SUN TZU AS IMMEDIATE and evocative for the English-speaking reader as it was for its Chinese lineage holders. Wherever possible, we have therefore recreated the experience of reading the *Sun Tzu* in Chinese. But the qualities of a text are more than words. They are also rhythm and structure, pacing and alternating patterns of obscurity and clear vista. To convey these we have reproduced qualities of the Chinese language that do not usually survive transposition into English.

Classical Chinese reads more slowly than the vernacular-based languages of the modern world. It has a blocky, measured rhythm, partway between our conceptions of poetry and prose. For example, the opening lines of the *Sun Tzu*:

ping che	The military
kuo chih ta-shih ye	is a great matter of the state.
ssu-sheng chih ti	It is the ground of death and life,
ts'un-wang chih tao	the Tao of survival or extinction.
pu-k'o pu-ch'a ye	One cannot but examine it.

Most of this is in four-word phrases—the *ye* at the end of lines two and five functions only to mark the finish of a sentence. The *Sun Tzu* freely mixes these four-word units with passages of irregular meter. Occasionally it uses rhyme, indicated in our translation by the symbol ∿. These rhymes function to structure lists of things, help the reader remember maxims or mark off the summary of a section or chapter. We cannot reproduce all these features in English, but we have sought to thicken our diction and employ the page-layout conventions of English poetry to convey something of their effect.

Like many translators, we maintain a single English equivalent for each Chinese word. For example, the word we have translated "military" has a range of meaning in Chinese that extends from "weapon" to "soldier" to "army" to the strategic thinking that underlies all of these. By rendering it consistently as "military," we rely on the reader to find the particular nuance that each context suggests while sustaining the larger field of meaning that unites them all.

This is not only for consistency. We use a single English word, rather than a phrase, for each Chinese word. Our goal is to preserve the lithic power of the text. For example, the *Sun Tzu* often compresses key insights into a single, potent aphorism:

The military is a Tao of deception. [Chapter 1]

Or:

Do not repeat the means of victory,
But respond to form from the inexhaustible.
     [Chapter 6]

Paraphrase would dilute this quality of the text and dissipate its energy. To avoid it, we have therefore been willing to accept an occasional awkwardness of expression. As a result, our translation uses only about 20 percent more words than the original. This compares favorably to the two-to-one ratio of many translations of classical Chinese, including those into the modern Chinese language.

The *Sun Tzu* is full of repetitions, parallel phrases and lists, phenomena that modern prose seeks to avoid. These suggest that the text has only recently emerged from the oral tradition. We have retained all these features, even when parallels in the text have caused us to extend the common meaning of English words or to invent new ones, such as *vincibility* as the opposite of *invincibility*. These allow us to better represent the thought processes of the original authors, their sense of the world's structuring. To do otherwise would distort the text in the guise of clarification, reducing it to some generic "clear meaning," like a prose translation of complex poetry.

We have therefore maintained the obscurities of the original, its compressed logic, its ambiguous connectors, its abrupt switches of point of view from "enemy" to "us." For example, the text says, "An army in chaos leads to victory" (chapter 3). It may take a moment to realize that my chaos is your victory, and vice versa. Again, a well-known rhymed couplet reads:

> Thus a small enemy's tenacity ∾
> Is a large enemy's catch. ∾ [Chapter 3]

This means that if we insist on fighting a larger foe, we will be captured by him.

Some of these difficulties have been so severe that editors in imperial times altered the text, substituting words or making internal connections more explicit. This is a common phenomenon in religious or philosophical texts, wherein the radical qualities of an early teaching are gradually obscured over the course of its transmission. As we excised later additions, we found an original form of the text with even greater power.

We were aided in this investigation by the 1972 recovery of a manuscript of the *Sun Tzu* written on bamboo in the early second century BCE. Though its variant forms affect only about 5 percent of the text, the readings of this bamboo manuscript are unexceptionally strong. Its cruder diction is close to the oral tradition from which the *Sun Tzu* had only recently emerged. As well, its military logic is often more profound than the standard text. We have therefore followed it wherever possible.

Our translation seeks as well to retain the rough edges of the text. To remove them is to strip the *Sun Tzu* of its texture and specificity. If we supply connectives missing in the original, we force smaller meanings on phrases that had been larger and more broadly applicable. Alternatively, we may misread relationships as closer than they appear to be. A common example is the word *ku*, which in most texts means "thus" or "therefore." In the *Sun Tzu*, however, it often occurs at the head of a section, joining two passages of apparently different origin.[1] Thus it marks a seam in the assemblage of the text rather than functioning as a logical connector. In these instances we have translated it "and so," rather than with the stronger "therefore."

It takes a Chinese reader as much time to resolve such difficulties as it does us. All classical texts have therefore been read with commentaries or even subcommentaries. These elucidate obscure words and establish authoritative meaning. The best known of them for the *Sun Tzu* is the *Ten-Man Notes*, the *Shih-chia chu*, which collects materials from the third to the eleventh centuries.

Our commentary supplies pieces that may be necessary to an English-speaking reader. However, our objective is less definitive interpretation than an opening of the text so that its greater meanings can be exposed. This is the same reasoning that led us to retain the structural features of the original. It derives from confidence that the reader will successfully negotiate such difficulties for himself or herself. It is important that any additions we make to the text be clearly identifiable, so that they may be dismantled and forgotten once the reader has found a more direct access to it.

Our translation relies almost exclusively on the *Sun Tzu* text and our knowledge of Warring States China. We have referred to commentaries like the *Ten-Man Notes*, but these reflect concerns of the imperial period and are thus not good guides to the original text. Throughout this work we have been guided by the writings of two great Chinese scholars, Yang Ping-an of the People's Liberation Army and Wu Chiu-lung of the Ministry of Culture, Beijing. Professor Yang is author of *Sun-tzu hui-chien* (1986), which discusses textual variants in considerable detail and also identifies numerous parallel passages in contemporary texts. Wu Chiu-lung led the 1972 archaeological expedition that excavated and deciphered the bamboo text. He is also senior author of the authoritative *Sun-tzu chiao-shih* (1990). Their work provides the sinological foundation for our book, and, like all students of Sun Tzu, we are in their debt.

We have sought, then, to create an English-language text that is immediately recognizable as itself. By standing a bit apart from everyday speech, it resists too ready an absorption into any preexisting world. We hope thereby to have opened up a ground on which the *Sun Tzu*'s original power can provoke the reader's own wisdom.

www.victoryoverwar.com

THIS BOOK IS PART OF A LARGER CONVERSATION. PUTTING IT IN print form has the unfortunate by-product of freezing the discussions at a particular point in their development. That is especially limiting for the *Sun Tzu*, since the text is above all a process. In order to keep that process alive, we have set up a Web site at www.victoryoverwar.com. It has the following features:

- A forum to discuss the text with other interested readers.

- A study guide with discussion topics and questions.

- Alternative essays that were born with the writing of this book but are represented in it only indirectly.

- The opportunity to examine the reasoning behind every choice made in this translation. These include decisions about the meaning range of Chinese words, a discussion of possible English equivalents and the weighing of textual variants. The site also includes the Chinese text of the *Sun Tzu*, with literal English equivalents supplied word by word. Altogether this constitutes the full scholarly apparatus for the book.

Please join us on the Web.

About the Denma Translation Group

THE DENMA TRANSLATION GROUP INCLUDES KIDDER SMITH, JAMES Gimian, Hudson Shotwell, Grant MacLean, Barry Boyce and Suzann Duquette. We worked together on the translation over a ten-year period. Kidder Smith and James Gimian served as general editors of the book and wrote the essays and commentary. Hudson Shotwell, Grant MacLean and Barry Boyce contributed to this writing in many ways. Grant MacLean composed the military history section of the essay "Joining the Tradition."

Kidder Smith teaches Chinese history at Bowdoin College, where he also directs the Asian Studies Program. He is senior author of *Sung Dynasty Uses of the I Ching* (Princeton, 1990) and has written on the military texts of ancient China. James Gimian is the publisher of the *Shambhala Sun* magazine and a publishing consultant. The other members of the group have worked professionally in the writing, editing and publication fields.

In the translation process we relied on the kind of material that is now available on our Web site, www.victoryoverwar.com. It contained the Chinese words of the text, their pronunciation and one or two English synonyms for each. Because Chinese and English word order is very similar, it was possible for non-Chinese speakers to follow the text in both languages. At first only Kidder Smith knew Chinese. Gradually, however, the group became familiar with a core of key words. These recurred often enough, and in varying contexts, for a set of highly nuanced understandings to emerge.

We argued over every word. What was its range of meaning in Chinese? To what extent was the proposed English word equivalent? Did the two have the same antonyms, and were they on the same level of formality? Above all, how much elasticity did the English language possess, that we could shape it into something that reflected the tone, style, cadence and pacing of the original Chinese? A few sentences of translation might require several hours of deliberation before a consensus would emerge.

Denma was a general of Gesar of Ling, the mythic warrior-king of Tibet. He is known as a skilled archer and master strategist. The Denma Translation Group was formed in 1991 to translate the *Sun Tzu*, but members of the group had already been studying the work for a decade. Each had received training in a contemplative discipline called the Dorje Kasung, which had been created by Chogyam Trungpa Rinpoche for Western students. This practice draws on the meditative and monastic traditions of Tibetan Buddhism, the Shambhala vision of an enlightened society, and some forms of the Western military traditions.

The *Sun Tzu* served as ideal study material for this discipline, as it showed taking whole and how to attain victory without battle. In this training we engaged the principles of the text in lifelike, intensified situations placed within a protected contemplative environment. Contemplative practice and *The Art of War* represent two very different traditions and disciplines. Yet both share the view that true victory is victory over aggression. We believe that it is the joining of these two disciplines that gives our translation its particular authority.

Acknowledgments

WE WOULD LIKE TO EXPRESS OUR THANKS TO:

Yang Ping-an and Wu Chiu-lung, whose pioneering work helped establish a working text, clarified the nature of its relationship with other early writings and integrated the bamboo text with traditional and modern scholarship on the *Sun Tzu*.

United States Marine Corps General Samuel B. Griffith, whose translation first communicated to us the core wisdom of the *Sun Tzu*.

David Mann, who worked with us on the translation during a number of early meetings.

David Graff, who offered impeccable advice at a key moment.

Jens Østergård Petersen, who provided an English version of *Krigskunsten*, his Danish translation of the *Sun Tzu*.

All those who read this book in manuscript and who offered important suggestions for its improvement: Willis Barnstone, Norman Cawse-Morgon, Dave Collings, Tom Conlan, Keith Cylar, Euan Davis, John DeMont, Bernie Flynn, June Knack, Melvin McLeod, Jens Østergård Petersen, Pat Robinson, David Rome and Jim Wheeler.

Carolyn Rose Gimian for her critical readings and editorial insight throughout the process.

Joe Spieler, for consistent counsel and sage advice.

Those many places in Nova Scotia that accommodated our

work over the years: Victory Communication, Trident Booksellers and Café, Dorje Denma Ling, Trident Mountain House and the Dunvegan cliffs of Cape Breton Island.

Our families, loved ones, partners and friends for their patience and support of our many long translation meetings and writing retreats.

Those members of the Western military who showed us the possibility of discipline and genuine warriorship.

Samuel Bercholz, Peter Turner, Jonathan Green, Joel Segel and the staff at Shambhala Publications for their enthusiastic support.

Our editor, Emily Hilburn Sell, for seeing so quickly what we were trying to do, for her confidence that we could do it and for her relentless sense of humor about the vicissitudes of life.

Michael Brackney, the indexer's indexer.

The early sessions of the Magyal Pomra Encampment and College of Denma, both training programs of the Dorje Kasung, where we were able to study the text and put into practice the wisdom of nonaggression in the midst of chaos.

And finally, the Vidyadhara Chögyam Trungpa Rinpoche, the Dorje Dradül of Mukpo, for the hard training and loving support, for his tireless generosity and dedication to all his students, whose unending compassion for sentient beings serves as the model for taking whole.

Any errors or misunderstandings are entirely our own.

Notes

Note to the Introduction

1. Samuel Griffith, *Sun Tzu—The Art of War* (Oxford, U.K.:
   Oxford University Press, 1963).

Notes to Part Two

Taking Whole

1. *Hsün Tzu*, Chapter 1.
2. For a further discussion of shih, see Roger T. Ames, "Strategic Advantage," in *Sun Tzu—The Art of Warfare* (New York:
   Ballantine, 1993).
3. P. Thompson, *The Shen Tzu Fragments* (Ann Arbor, Mich.:
   University Microfilms, 1970), 516.
4. *Lord Shang*, chapter 24.

Joining the Tradition

1. See Mark Edward Lewis, *Writing and Authority in Early China*
   (Albany: State University of New York Press, 1999).
2. For the best analysis of these processes, see Mark Edward
   Lewis, *Sanctioned Violence in Early China* (Albany: State
   University of New York Press, 1990).

3. See the translation by Ralph Sawyer, *The Seven Military Classics of Ancient China* (Boulder, Colo.: Westview Press, 1993).

4. See *Records of the Historian*, translated by Yang Hsien-yi and Gladys Yang (Hong Kong: Commercial Press, 1974), 28–29.

5. For an excellent discussion of this process, see "Writing the Masters," in Lewis, *Writing and Authority in Early China*.

6. These have been translated by Roger Ames as "Texts Recovered from Later Works," in his *Sun Tzu—The Art of Warfare* (New York: Ballantine, 1993).

7. See Thomas Petzinger, *The New Pioneers* (New York: Simon and Schuster, 1999), and www.cluetrain.com.

8. From T. E. Lawrence, "The Evolution of a Revolt," quoted by Alex Danchev in "Liddell-Hart and the Indirect Approach," *Journal of Military History* 63 (April 1999): 329–30.

9. Quoted in Samuel B. Griffith, *Sun Tzu—The Art of War* (Oxford, U.K.: Oxford University Press, 1963), v.

10. Quoted in Phillip B. Davidson, *Vietnam at War* (Novato, Calif.: Presidio Press, 1988), 15.

11. From Lawrence, "Evolution of a Revolt," quoted by Danchev in "Liddell-Hart and the Indirect Approach," 330.

12. U.S. Marine Corps, *Warfighting (MCDP 1)* (Washington, D.C.: U.S. Department of the Navy, 1997).

Notes to Part Three

Chapter 3: Strategy of Attack

1. See the discussion in Wu Chiu-lung, *Sun Tzu chiao-shih* (Beijing: 1990), 42.

Chapter 9: Moving the Army

1. See Lewis, *Sanctioned Violence in Early China*; and Michael Puett, "Sages, Ministers, and Rebels," *Harvard Journal of Asiatic Studies* 58 (1998): 425–79.

Chapter 11: The Nine Grounds

1. A panoramic history of China by Ssu-ma Ch'ien, written in the years around 100 BCE. See the translation of these stories by Burton Watson in *Records of the Historian* (New York: Columbia University Press, 1958), chapter 86, pp. 45–48.

Chapter 12: Attack by Fire

1. See Joseph Needham and Robin D. S. Yates, *Science and Civilisation in China*, vol. 5, pt. 6 (Cambridge, U.K.: Cambridge University Press, 1994), 463 ff.
2. See John Keegan, *A History of Warfare* (New York: Knopf, 1993).
3. Colin A. Ronan, *The Shorter Science and Civilisation in China*, vol. 2 (Cambridge, U.K.: Cambridge University Press, 1981), 92.
4. See *The Intrigues of the Warring States*, translated by J. I. Crump as *Chan-kuo ts'e* (San Francisco: Chinese Materials Center, 1979), 278–82.

Note to About the Translation

1. See Robin D. S. Yates, "New Light on Ancient Chinese Military Texts," *T'oung Pao* 74 (1988): 219.

Index

Page numbers in bold italics refer to the *Sun Tzu* text.

facing death: and bravery, **48–49**, 202–4
fascicles (book bundles), 113
fate star, 8, **21**, 139, 159
fearlessness of the sage commander, xiv–xv
feeding the army, 7, 8, 137, 138
fellowship: unifying soldiers by, **38**, 187
feudal lords, 136
    controlling, **31**, **52**, 176, 209
    not knowing, **26**, **52**, 168, 209
    troubles from, 7, **11**, 136, 144
the few: striking the many with, **22**, 161
fighting. *See* doing battle
fire: attack by, **55–57**, 213–17
the five (factors), **3–4**, 127–30, 131
five advantages, **31**, **52**, 176, 209
five dangers for the general, **32**, 177
Five Phases: cycle of, **24**, 164–65
five pitches/colors/tastes, **17–18, 19,**
    153–55, 157
fixations, as impediments, 77–78
    See also character excesses
flags and pennants, **27**, 170
flexibility: formlessness and, **23–24,**
    80–81, 164
following up on victory, **56**, 215–16
force, 83
    use of, xvii, 136, 137
foreknowledge (of spies), **59, 60,**
    219–20, 221, 222, 223, 224
form (shape), **13–15**, 79, 146–50, 156
    as formlessness, **23**, 80, 163
    knowing, 79
    of the military, **23–24**, 80–81, 163, 164
    relying on, **23**, 79, 163
    responding to, **23**, 79, 86, 163
    shih as, 72
    of victory, **23**, 79, 163
forming, 79
    See also shaping the ground
formlessness
    form as, **23**, 80, 163
    of the general, **21**, **50**, 160–61, 206
    power of, **21**, **23**, 159–60, 163
forms of the earth, **40–44**, 188–96
Four Emperors, 180
freedom of action, 93–95, 97, 99
friction (opposition), 84

gender usage in the *Sun Tzu*, xiv
general (sage commander), xiv, **4**, 64,
    82–106, 129

activity, **50**, 93–99, 206–7
awesomeness, **52**, 93–94, 101, 210
calamities of leadership, **41–42**, 191–93
and chaos, **18**, **42**, **43**, 90–93, 155–56,
    192, 195
consistency, **38–39**, 187
and the contending army, **25**, 166
discipline, 88–89
employing, **4**, 131
excesses of character, **32**, **43–44**,
    77–78, 177, 195
exertion (energy), **44**, 88–89, 195–96
and the extraordinary, **16–17**, **47**,
    105–6, 153, 202
fearlessness, xiv–xv
formlessness, **21**, **50**, 160–61, 206
freedom of action, 93–95, 97
gentleness, 87
image, 82–83
inquisitiveness, 87, 88
inscrutability, **50**, 206
invisibility, **21**, **50**, 98–99, 159–60, 206
killing the enemy general, **32**, **53**, 94,
    177, 211
kinship with his troops. *See* kinship
knowledge of the military, 139, 168,
    175–76, 193, 209
loyalty to, **43**, **49–50**, 87–88, 194, 207
power images, **27**, 169
power source, xiv, 86, 95–97
problem resolution, 92–93
purpose (intention), **43**, 93, 95, 186,
    194
qualities (being of), xiv, **4**, 86–89, 93,
    129
and the ruler, 8, **43**, **55**, 139, 194, 216
skill, **15**, **53**, 149, 211
and spies, **58**, **61**, 219, 222, 223, 224
and the state, 8, **11**, **43**, 87, 139, 143,
    194
Tao of, **43**, 193
toughness of command, **53**, 93–95,
    210–11
trouble signs in, **37–38**, 185–86
trust in himself, xiv, **52**, 86–87, 91,
    95, 210
trust of others in, 87–88
vs. tyrant, 94–95
and victory, 93–95, 96–97, 99–106
weakness in, **42**, 90, 192
wisdom, xiv–xv, 82
gentleness of the sage commander, 87

employing. *See* method
form, **23–24**, 80–81, 163, 164
  as a great matter of the state, 3, 127
  heaven and, **3–4**, 89, 128–29
  knowing, 8, **44**, 139, 195–96
  knowledge of, 139, 168, 175–76, 193, 209
  long-lasting battle and, **6–7**, 136
  method. *See* method
  not knowing the harm from employing, 7, 136–37
  objectives not to be pursued, **30**, 175
  power images, **27**, 169
  practices in ancient China, 108, 109–10
  prevailing through preponderance, **16**, 152
  purpose, 83–84
  skill. *See* skill of the general
  superior vs. inferior militaries, **10**, 141
  Tao of, **3**, 128
  transformation of, **27**, 168
  and victory, 8, 139
  in the Warring States period, 109–10
  See also army; officers; soldiers
military lineage: victories of, xvi, **5**, 99, 110, 123, 133
military thinking: contemporary: and the *Sun Tzu* tradition, 119–22
mind: contemplative, 85
modern warfare
  and fire, 213
  military thinking, 119–22
moon: phase cycles, **24**, 164–65
"more is not better," **38**, 186
the mountain collapsing calamity, **42**, 192
mountain image, **19**, 73, 157
mountains: crossing, **33**, 178
movements (of energy)
  as Tao, 80–81
  things as, 77
moving the army, **33–39**, 178–87
  arriving for battle sooner, **20**, **25**, 158, 167
  not knowing the ground, **26**, **52**, 168, 209
  across terrain and water, **33–35**, 178–81
  See also advancing

narrow form of the earth, **41**, 189–90
native spy (local spy), **59**, **60**, 220, 222

natural cycles, **24**, **28**, 164–65, 171
natural science: and the *Sun Tzu* tradition, 118
natural world. *See* world
nature of things, 65–67, 69
  rocks and trees, **18–19**, 73, 76–77, 86, 157
  See also relationships among things
nine grounds, **45–54**, 197–212
  as not exhaustive, 200
  types, **45–46**, **51–52**, 197–200, 207–8
nine transformations, **30–32**, 174–77, 176
node (of shih), **17–18**, 71, 72, 154–55
not knowing
  and defeat, **12**, 145
  the enemy, **42**, **58**, 192–93, 218
  the feudal lords, **26**, **52**, 168, 209
  the ground, **26**, **52**, 168, 209
  the harm from employing the military, 7, 136–37

objectives not to be pursued, **30**, 175
objects. *See* things
offering advantage (choices), **18**, **20**, **25**, 101, 156, 158, 166–67
officers
  bravery, **48–49**, 203–4
  strength facing death, **48**, 202–3
  weakness in, **42**, 191
  wrath in a great officer, **42**, 192
  See also soldiers
omens: prohibiting, **48**, 203
oneself
  being. *See* being: of the sage commander
  concern with, 78, 86, 93
  knowing, xii–xiii, **12**, 44, 95, 96, 145, 195, 196
  positioning, 68, 178
  relying on, **31**, 99, 177
  trust in, xiv, **52**, 86–87, 91, 95, 210
open form of the earth, **40**, 188
opposition (friction), 84
oral traditions: function, 76
ordering
  ch'i, **28**, 170–71
  heart-mind, **28**, 171
  the many, **16**, 151
  strength, **28**, 171
  transformation, **28**, 172
orders. *See* commands of the ruler

on form, 23, 79, 163
on oneself, 31, 99, 177
on shih, 18–19, 73–74, 156–57
responding
    to aggression, xii–xiii, xvi–xvii, 84, 100
    to approach, 47, 201
    to chaos, 84, 90–93
    to conflict, xii–xiii, xvi–xvii, 92–93
    to crises, 84
    to form, 23, 79, 86, 163
retreat, 21, 160
reversing conditions, 166–67
rhyming passages in the text, 1, 132
river Chin: diversion of, 215
rocks: nature and image of, 18–19, 73,
    76–77, 86, 157
rod-counting before battle, 5, 132
routed calamity, 42, 192
ruler (sovereign)
    adversarial acts toward the army, 11, 144
    commands. See commands of the ruler
    and the general, 8, 43, 55, 139, 194, 216
    power, 70
rush of water image, 17, 72, 154

sage commander. See general
sages: and spies, 60, 221
salt marshes: crossing, 34, 179
scrutinizing the enemy, 33, 35–38, 178,
    181–86
searching through cover, 35, 181
seasons
    cycle of, 24, 164
    for setting fires, 55, 214
secrecy: of spies, 59, 60, 221
security. See protection of the state
seed: knowing, 96
seeds and wind image, 77
seizing loved things, 47, 54, 201, 212
self. See oneself
self-concern: large view and, 78, 86, 93
self-discipline. See discipline of the sage
    commander
self-interest: trust in, 52, 210
self-knowledge. See knowing: oneself
self-reliance, 31, 99, 177
setting fires, 55, 56, 214, 215
Seven Pillars of Wisdom (Lawrence), 121
shape. See form
shaping the ground, 97, 156
    cultivating shih, 69, 71, 86, 91–92, 103

of invincibility, 13, 146
methods, 101–3
of no defeat, 14, 99–101, 147, 148
for taking whole, 104
See also the circuitous and direct;
    deception; transforming with
    the enemy
shih, 5, 16–19, 63, 70–76, 86, 131–32,
    151–57
aspects (facets), 71–73
chaos and, 91–92
circumstances and, 70–71, 73, 76–77
cultivating, 69, 71, 86, 91–92, 103.
    See also shaping the ground
forms. See ground: types
images, 17–18, 19, 72–73, 153–55, 157
knowing, 43, 80, 193
learning, 74–76, 80
as of the moment, 74, 134, 191
the node, 17–18, 71, 72, 154–55
relying on, 18–19, 73–74, 156–57
striking when equal in, 42, 191
and victory, 74, 133, 156–57
See also power; preponderance
shuai-jan image, 49, 204–5
siege, 10, 141
of Chin-yang, 215
defense against, 55, 213
See also walled cities
signals in battle, 27, 170
signs
of the enemy, 35–37, 182–84
of trouble with the general, 37–38,
    185–86
situations. See circumstances
skill of the general, 14–15, 53, 146,
    147–49, 211
at battle, 10, 14, 21, 142, 147–48, 159
skillful action, xv–xvi, 67–69, 78–79,
    92–93, 94–95, 97
key to. See shih
See also activity of the sage com-
    mander; skill of the general
soldiers (troops)
binding/commanding, 53, 94, 210–11
impoverishment from, 7–8, 58, 66,
    137–38, 218
kinship with the general. See kinship
ordering the many, 16, 151
strength facing death, 48, 202–3
throwing in death ground, 48, 53,
    202–3, 210–11

vs. destroying, 9–10, 65, 140–42
discerning the purpose of the enemy,
    53, 211
shaping the ground, 104
swiftness in, 104–5
and victory, 9, 10, 140–41, 142, 145
Tao, 79, 80–81, 128, 149
    chaos as, 79
    of the circuitous and direct, 25, 27,
        102–3, 166–67, 169–70
    of a contending army, 169–70
    of deception, 5, 132–33, 163
    of defeat, 42, 193
    of the earth, 41, 190–91
    of the general, 43, 193
    of governance, 49, 152, 205
    of the invader, 47–48, 202
    knowing. See knowing Tao
    of knowing victory, xv, 12, 144–45
    of the military, 3, 81, 128
    movement as, 80–81
    of spies, 59, 123, 220
    of water, 81
tea pouring story, 85
teaching modes of the Sun Tzu, 74–76, 85
tears: and bravery, 48–49, 203–4
tendencies of things, 69
terrain. See ground
things (details)
    as changing, 24, 69, 71, 76–77,
        164–65
    interconnectedness, 66
    interdependence, 66–67, 67–69, 76–77
    knowing, 65–66, 79, 95, 96
    love of goods: and bravery, 48–49, 203–4
    as movements, 77
    nature of, 65–67, 69
    shaping. See deception
    tendencies, 69
    the way things work, 79, 81
    See also circumstances; world
three armies, 144
timing (the moment)
    knowing the time of battle, 22,
        161–62
    the node, 17–18, 71, 72, 154–55
    setting fires, 56, 215
    See also waiting
toughness of the sage commander, 93–95
tradition of the Sun Tzu. See Sun Tzu
    tradition
transformation (change)

of the military, 27, 168
the nine transformations, 30–32, 174–77
ordering, 28, 172
of things, 24, 69, 71, 76–77, 164–65
transforming with the enemy, 18, 21, 24,
    54, 81, 97, 101–3, 156, 160–61,
    164, 172, 211
    See also the circuitous and direct;
        deception; shaping the ground
translation, strategy for, xx, 116–17
transmitting victory: as impossible, xvi,
    5, 99, 110, 123, 133
trees: nature of, 18–19, 86, 157
trench warfare: and contemporary mili-
    tary thinking, 119
troops. See soldiers
trouble with the general: signs of, 37–38,
    185–86
trust of the sage commander
    in himself, xiv, 52, 86–87, 91, 95, 210
    in others, 87–88
Ts'ao Kuei, 49, 204
turned spy, 59, 60, 61, 220, 222, 223

U.S. Marine Corps: Warfighting manual,
    121–22
uncertainty. See chaos
the unexpected. See the extraordinary
unifying soldiers
    in battle, 28, 49, 170, 205
    by fellowship, 38, 187

vegetation: searching through, 35, 181
victory, xvi, 5, 13, 99, 106, 133, 146
    over aggression, xvii, 100, 106
    avoiding danger to, 44, 196
    as before battle, 14, 100, 148
    without battle, xviii, 9, 10, 84, 141, 142
    complete (true), xvii–xviii, 44, 96, 196
    vs. conquest, 175
    determining the means for, xvi
    following up on, 56, 215–16
    form, 23, 79, 163
    half of, 44, 195
    heaven and, 4, 130
    increasing strength through, 8, 139
    knowing. See knowing victory
    knowledge and, 4, 12, 130, 145
    long-lasting, 6–7, 136
    making. See making victory

victory (*continued*)
    measure of, **15**, 149
    method, **15**, 149
    and the military, **8**, 139
    of the military lineage, xvi, **5**, 99, 133
    as of the moment, xvi, 99
    preponderance and, **15**, **16**, 38, 103,
        150, 152, 186
    rejecting parts of, xviii, 106
    the sage commander and, 93–95,
        96–97, 99–106
    shih and, 74, 133, 156–57
    skill in, **14**, 147–48
    of the *Sun Tzu* in EuroAmerican
        culture, 122–23
    taking whole and, **9**, **10**, 140–41, 142,
        145
    transmitting as impossible, xvi, **5**, 99,
        110, 123, 133
    turning defeat into, **53**, 210–11
    usurped, **23**, 162
    over war, 106
    weighing, **15**, 149, 150
    as win-win, xviii
Vietnam War: and the *Sun Tzu* tradi-
        tion, 120–21
views. *See* large view
vincibility, **13**, 146
virtues: excesses of, **32**, **43–44**, 77–78,
        177, 195
Vo Nguyen Giap: military thinking, 121

waiting
    awaiting chaos/clamor, or difficulty,
        28, 92, 171
    at stream crossings, **34**, 181
walled cities
    attacking, **6**, **10**, 136, 141
    defeating, **10**, **52**, 142, 210
    See also siege
war
    initial measures, **53**, 211
    modern warfare, 213
    victory over, 106
    See also battle
Warfighting manual (U.S. Marine
        Corps), 121–22
Warring States period China, 109–11
water
    crossing, **33**, 179
    movement, **23–24**, 80–81, 164

power of diversion, **56**, 215
rush of, **17**, 72, 154
Tao of, 81
Way. *See* Tao
the way things work, 79, 81
    See also Tao
ways of being, **27**, 169
weakness
    in the general/officers/soldiers, **42**, 90,
        191–92
    and strength, **18**, 155
weapons: dividing captured resources,
        27, 169
weather. *See* heaven
Web site: translators', xxi–xxii, 117, 230
weighing victory, **15**, 149, 150
Whitehead, Alfred North: process
        philosophy, 119
will to live: danger of, **32**, 177
willingness to die: danger of, **32**, 177
win-win: victory as, xv
winning. *See* victory
wisdom
    individual: empowering, xiii
    as our own, xvi, xxii
    of the sage commander, xiv–xv, 82
    of the *Sun Tzu*, xii, xiv, xvi, xxii, 63,
        122
    See also knowing; knowledge
world (natural world)
    action in. *See* action
    complexity, 71
    cycles, **24**, **28**, 164–65, 171
    fourfold division, 182
    mastering, 205
    power images, **27**, 169
    See also things
wrath, **57**, 216
    in a great officer, **42**, 192
    raising an army out of, **56**, **57**, 216
    See also anger; rancor
Wu, **23**, **49**, 162, 204–5

yang, **34**, 180
Yellow Emperor, **34**, 180
yin, **27**, **34**, 169, 180
Yueh, **23**, **49**, 162, 204–5

Zen story: pouring tea, 85
zone, xiii, 85